A Multi-scale Assessment and Evaluation of Historic Openlands at Sleeping Bear Dunes National Lakeshore

Natural Resource Technical Report NPS/GLKN/NRTR—2009/150

I0426257

R. Gregory Corace, III[1]
Integrated Land Management Services
39234N Fisherman's Lane
Chassell, MI 49916

P. Charles Goebel
School of Natural Resources
Ohio Agricultural Research and Development Center
The Ohio State University
1680 Madison Avenue
Wooster, OH 44691

and

Thomas C. Wyse
School of Natural Resources
Ohio Agricultural Research and Development Center
The Ohio State University
1680 Madison Avenue
Wooster, OH 44691

Current Address:
[1] Seney National Wildlife Refuge
1674 Refuge Entrance Rd.
Seney, MI 49883
Greg_Corace@fws.gov

January 2009

U.S. Department of the Interior
National Park Service
Natural Resource Program Center
Fort Collins, Colorado

The Natural Resource Publication series addresses natural resource topics that are of interest and applicability to a broad readership in the National Park Service and to others in the management of natural resources, including the scientific community, the public, and the NPS conservation and environmental constituencies. Manuscripts are peer-reviewed to ensure that the information is scientifically credible, technically accurate, appropriately written for the intended audience, and is designed and published in a professional manner.

The Natural Resources Technical Reports series is used to disseminate the peer-reviewed results of scientific studies in the physical, biological, and social sciences for both the advancement of science and the achievement of the National Park Service's mission. The reports provide contributors with a forum for displaying comprehensive data that are often deleted from journals because of page limitations. Current examples of such reports include the results of research that addresses natural resource management issues; natural resource inventory and monitoring activities; resource assessment reports; scientific literature reviews; and peer reviewed proceedings of technical workshops, conferences, or symposia.

Views, statements, findings, conclusions, recommendations and data in this report are solely those of the author(s) and do not necessarily reflect views and policies of the U.S. Department of the Interior, NPS. Mention of trade names or commercial products does not constitute endorsement or recommendation for use by the National Park Service.

Printed copies of reports in these series may be produced in a limited quantity and they are only available as long as the supply lasts. This report is also available from the Natural Resource Publications Management website (http://www.nature.nps.gov/publications/NRPM) on the Internet or by sending a request to the address on the back cover.

Please cite this publication as:

Corace, R. G., III, P. C. Goebel, and T. C. Wyse. 2009. A multi-scale assessment and evaluation of historic openlands at Sleeping Bear Dunes National Lakeshore. Natural Resource Technical Report NPS/GLKN/NRTR—2009/150. National Park Service, Fort Collins, Colorado.

NPS D-128, January 2009

Contents

Figures

Tables

Appendixes

Abstract

Throughout much of North America populations of openland (grassland-shrubland-early successional forests) birds have been declining dramatically, primarily in response to the loss of available habitat. In the Upper Midwest, some lands managed by the National Park Service, such as those at Sleeping Bear Dunes National Lakeshore, contain historic cultural openlands that may provide important habitat for some openland bird species. With this in mind, we characterized the plant and bird communities of historic openlands (fields) of Sleeping Bear Dunes National Lakeshore at multiple scales. At the Lakeshore scale, we characterized the openland bird community and produced an ordinal scaling of abundance based on the frequency of encountering each species. We found the bird community associated with these openlands to be comprised of 13 openland species of conservation priority as deemed by the United States Fish and Wildlife Service Region Three (Midwest): black-billed cuckoo, bobolink, Connecticut warbler, eastern meadowlark, field sparrow, grasshopper sparrow, Henslow's sparrow, Le Conte's sparrow, northern harrier, sedge wren, upland sandpiper, western meadowlark, whip-poor-will. We then investigated long-term population trend data for all bird species encountered to assess on a relative basis the conservation value of openland habitats. At the field scale, we delineated the boundaries and quantified the spatial characteristics (e.g., area, perimeter, edge type) of 12 fields currently managed under the Lakeshore's Meadow Management Plan. Additionally, we characterized the overstory and ground-flora vegetation of the major habitat types (e.g., building edge, field edge, field interior, forest edge, forest interior) associated with each field. The results of these analyses suggest that the composition and structure of the overstory and ground-flora plant communities of the building edge, field edge, and field interior habitat types are similar, while the forest edge and forest interior habitats are reflective of either a sugar maple-red oak forest type or a sugar maple-beech-eastern hemlock forest type. Finally, we estimated the density of birds inhabiting these fields and related these values to habitat structure and composition. Our analyses suggest that the density of many openland species is regulated by the interaction of field size, shape, and edge type. Based on the findings of this study and ongoing openland assessments at larger spatial scales, we suggest that maintaining the larger or more contiguous patches of these historic openlands will benefit local, state, and regional (Upper Midwest) populations of openland birds.

Acknowledgements

We wish to thank several individuals whose help proved invaluable for this project. We would like to express our gratitude to Max Holden and Steve Yancho for their help in selecting research sites and providing logistical support. Without their assistance, this research would not have been possible. We also wish to thank Kim Struthers for her support in acquiring many of the spatial data layers and help managing the spatial data collected over the course of this study. Additional help with acquiring USDA Forest Service data was provided by Kim Brosofske. Susan Coller assisted with field data collection and mapping. We also wish to thank several individuals from the Ohio Agricultural Research and Development Center who provided field assistance and critical reviews of earlier versions of this report: Clay Dygert, Katie Holmes and Marie Semko-Duncan; Holly Petrillo (University of Michigan) also provided editorial assistance. Finally, we would like to acknowledge the editorial comments of Bill Route, Joan Elias, and Karin Kozie that helped refine the focus of this work.

Introduction

The policy of the National Park Service (NPS) directs land managers to maintain "natural [ecosystem] components and processes in their natural condition," and where human activities have altered significantly these natural biological and physical processes, to "restore them to a natural condition or to maintain the closest approximation of the natural condition in situations in which a truly natural system is no longer attainable" (National Park Service 2001). Generally, the "natural condition" is considered to be the spectrum of ecosystem conditions (including ecosystem composition, structure, and function) occurring within a defined area over a specified period of time prior to European settlement (Landres et al. 1999; Moore et al. 1999; Allen et al. 2002). However, there has been an increasing awareness in the NPS of the importance of NPS-defined historic cultural landscapes. And in some instances, the maintenance of these human-modified landscapes has been considered an acceptable management scenario. At Sleeping Bear Dunes National Lakeshore (hereafter referred to as the Lakeshore) historic cultural openlands (grassland-shrubland-early successional forests on lands that were once in agricultural production) provide such a management conundrum.

To understand the potential predicament in which the NPS finds itself, it is important to understand the past and present conditions of the Lakeshore because the human history of the Lakeshore has had a profound influence on which plant and bird species inhabit the current landscape. Before Europeans arrived, the area associated with the Lakeshore was dominated by a beech-sugar maple-hemlock cover type (Table 1; Figure 1). (Common and scientific names of all bird species discussed are listed in Appendix A; scientific names for all plants are listed in Appendix B.) During the late 19th and early 20th centuries, extensive timber harvesting was followed by considerable agricultural land conversion. However, except for fruit production, poor soil conditions thwarted economically viable farming (Karamanski 2000). In 1919, a small portion of what is now the Lakeshore was set aside as a State Park. The idea of a National Park in northwestern Michigan did not surface until the NPS's Great Lakes Shoreline Survey visited the area in 1958. This culminated in the creation of Sleeping Bear Dunes National Lakeshore 12 years later, in 1970 (Karamanski 2000). More than 1,400 tracts of private land, many of which were small local farms, were acquired to create the Lakeshore. The result is a patchwork of vegetation and habitat that does not necessarily reflect the natural conditions.

Table 1. Distribution of pre-European settlement vegetation at Sleeping Bear Dunes National Lakeshore.

Forest type	Area (ha)	% of Landscape
Beech-Sugar Maple-Hemlock	16,767.64	69.7
Sand Dunes	1,740.47	7.2
Mixed-Conifer Swamps	1,676.32	7.0
White Pine-Red Pine	1,510.05	6.3
Hemlock-White Pine	1,196.94	5.0
Northern White Cedar Swamps	348.91	1.5
Jack Pine-Red Pine	288.58	1.2
Shrub Swamp and Emergent Marshes	90.73	<1.0
Mixed Hardwood Swamps	9.56	<0.1
Aspen-Birch	2.91	<0.1
Lakes and Rivers	431.38	1.8
Total	24,063.50	100.0

As land conversion has shaped the area encompassed by the Lakeshore, human land use has likewise altered native openlands throughout North America. In particular, the amount of native prairie habitat has declined drastically and both natural secondary succession in the absence of fire and active reforestation and succession have altered the composition and structure of shrubland habitats (Askins 2000). Consequently, long-term Breeding Bird Survey (BBS) population trend data and other information from different geographic regions of North America suggest alarming trends for many of 28 species considered grassland obligates (Sauer et al. 2001). Although relatively less studied, many of the 86 bird species that typically utilize shrublands and early successional stages of forest development are also declining at high rates (Sauer et al. 2001). Not surprisingly, when this information is placed into a bird conservation scenario for Michigan, one finds that 28% of the state's species of conservation concern are associated with openland (i.e., grassland and successional-scrub) habitats (Figure 2).

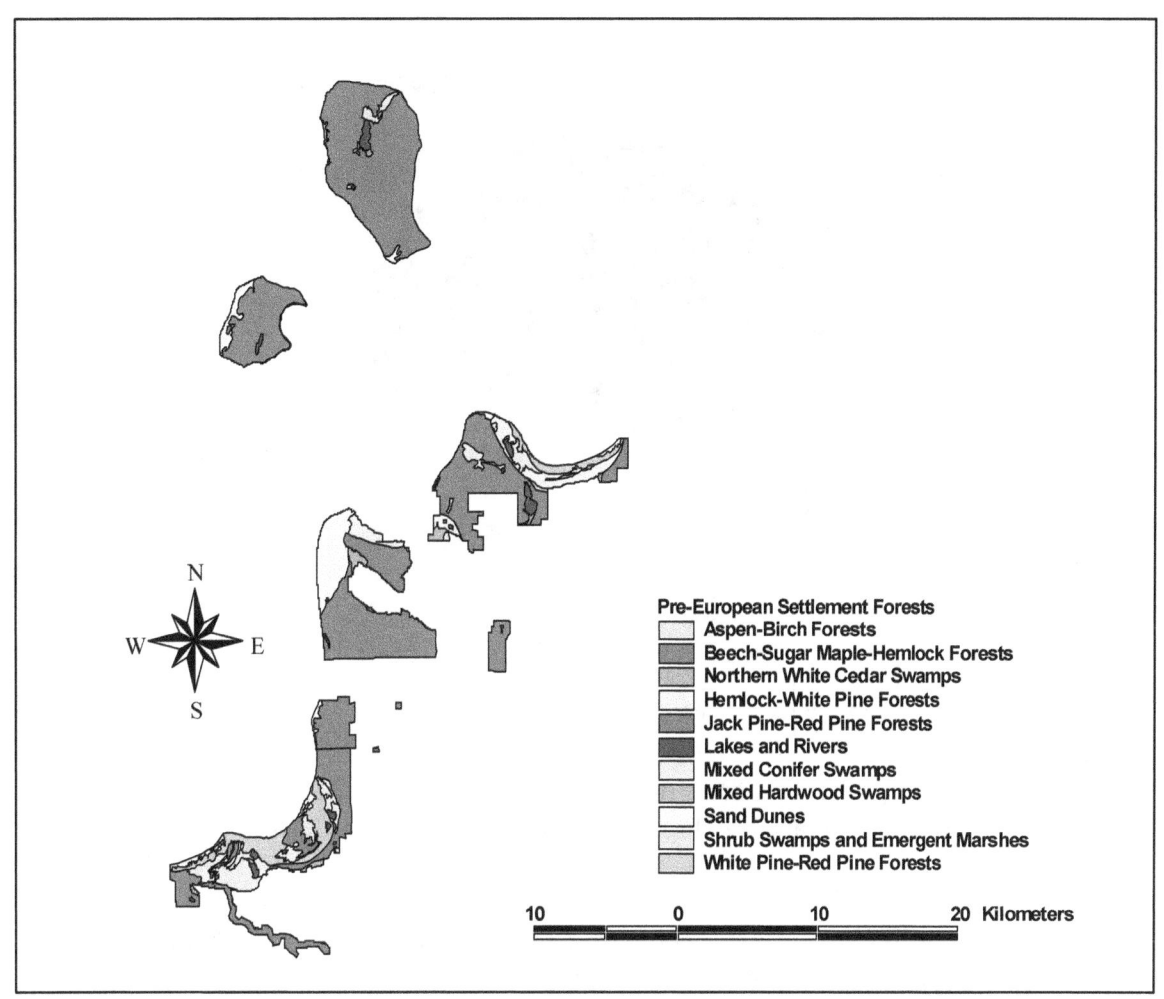

Figure 1. Pre-European settlement vegetation of Sleeping Bear Dunes National Lakeshore based on interpretations of General Land Office (GLO) survey notes.

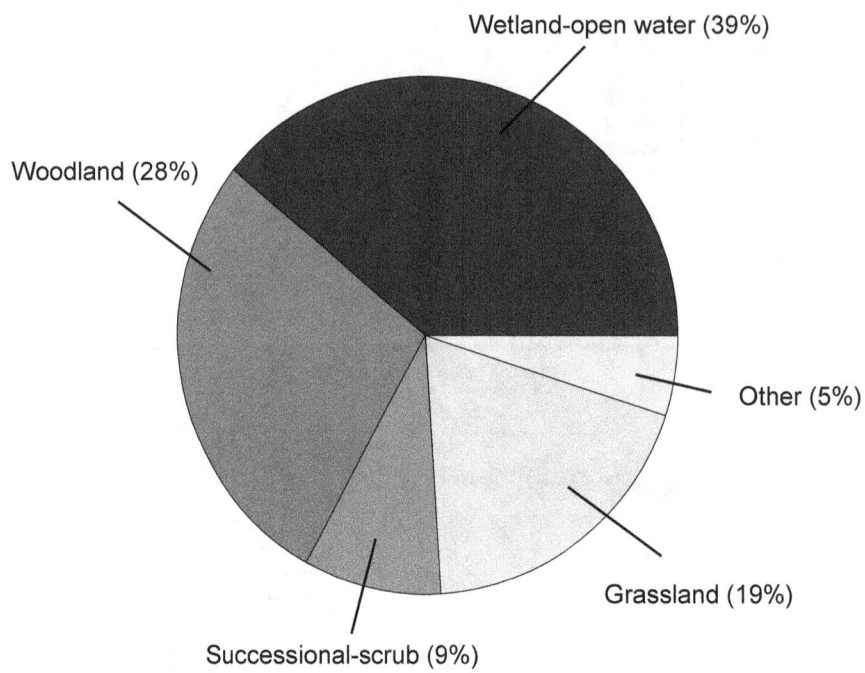

Figure 2. Percentage of 43 bird species listed as endangered, threatened, and special concern in Michigan by breeding habitat (Michigan Department of Natural Resources 1999).

According to the Lakeshore's Historic Properties Management Plan and Environmental Impact Statement (EIS), the NPS has targeted historic sites at the Lakeshore for preservation. These areas represent a significant portion of the 458 fields currently distributed across the Lakeshore and have been managed under guidelines set out in the Lakeshore's draft Meadow Management Plan, a plan designed to maintain the open features of these historic and culturally significant agricultural landscapes.

In this report we assess and evaluate openland habitats at the Lakeshore and field scales and, in doing so, build upon the prior research of Scharf (1997) and the multi-scale assessment work of Corace (2007). We focus our efforts on understanding the ecological contributions provided by these habitats for openland bird species of conservation concern. Our top-down analysis provides us with a framework to assess the conservation status of individual ecosystems at the Lakeshore and prioritize efforts within the context of contemporary environmental issues, such as the decline in populations of openland bird species across the Upper Midwest (i.e., Michigan, Minnesota, and Wisconsin). Specifically, in this report we address the following questions:

1. What are the spatial characteristics of the Lakeshore's openlands?
2. What species comprise the vegetation communities of the Lakeshore's openlands?
3. What bird species inhabit the openlands at Lakeshore and individual field scales?
4. What are the population trends and status of bird species encountered?
5. What factors (e.g., vegetation composition and structure, field size) influence bird communities in fields?
6. What is the potential role of the Lakeshore's openlands when considered in the broader context of openland habitat availability throughout the Upper Midwest?

Study Area

Sleeping Bear Dunes National Lakeshore is located along the northeastern shore of Lake Michigan (Figure 3). The Lakeshore stretches approximately 63.5 km along the Lake Michigan shoreline and includes two islands: North and South Manitou islands. The Lakeshore is almost entirely in the Manistee Subsection (VII.4) of the Northern Lacustrine-influenced Lower Michigan Section (VII), a glacially-modified landscape dominated by steep, narrow moraines and flat sandy lake plains with elevations from 177 m to 350 m (Albert 1995). The most prominent features of the Lakeshore, and those for which it is named, are the perched dunes on glacial moraines approximately 100 to 125 m above Lake Michigan. Dominant dune vegetation includes buffalo berry, ground juniper, and jack pine (Thompson 1967).

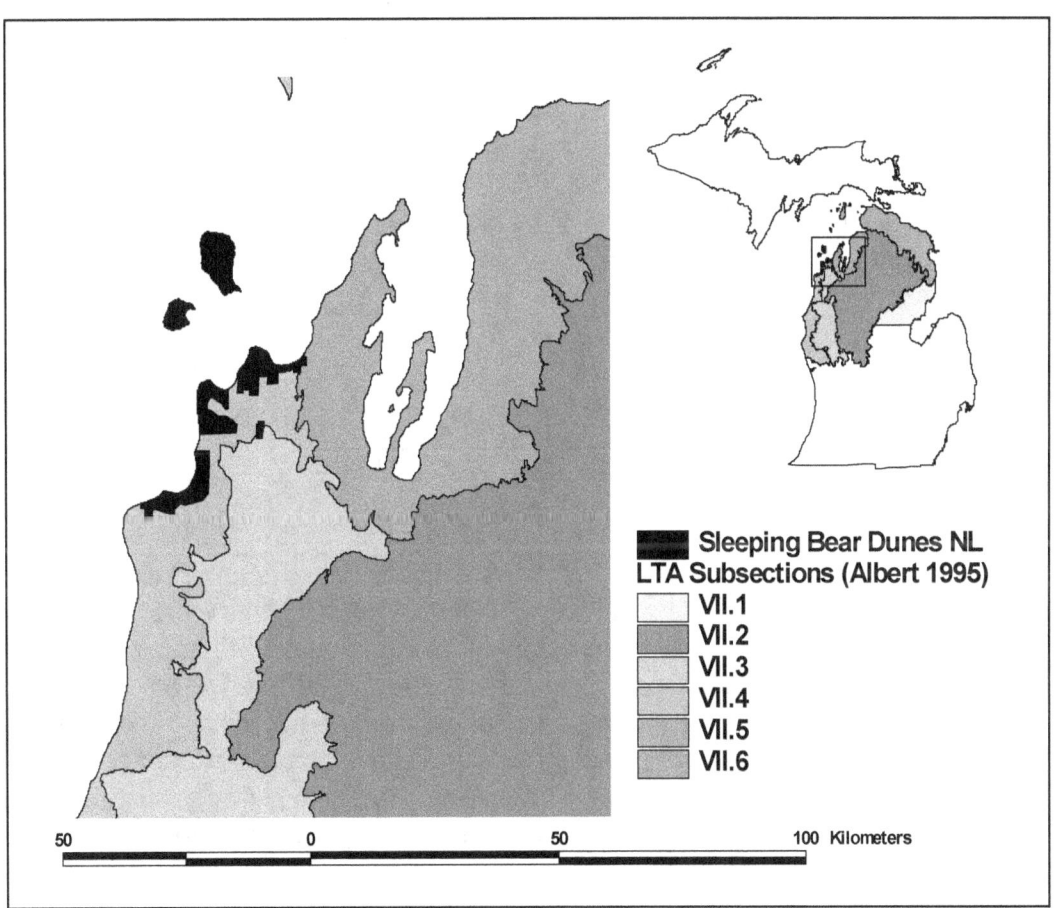

Figure 3. Location and landtype associations of northern Michigan and Sleeping Bear Dunes National Lakeshore (Albert 1995).

In addition to the dunes, the Lakeshore contains a variety of forest ecosystems, including mixed oak-pine forests on more sandy sites, swamp hardwood and conifer forests on poorly drained soils, and upland northern hardwood-hemlock forests. The extensive northern hardwood-hemlock forests across the upland areas of the Lakeshore are due to the maritime influence of

5

Lake Michigan. The Lakeshore receives between 76 and 84 cm of precipitation per year, has moderate temperatures (annual average of 6°C), and experiences a growing season of between 140 to 150 days per year (Albert 1995). In contrast, areas more inland in northern Lower Michigan experience lower annual precipitation, much cooler temperatures, and a shorter growing season (Albert 1995). Detailed descriptions and maps of the current vegetation of the Lakeshore were developed by Hazlett (1986) (Table 2; Figure 4).

Table 2. Distribution of current vegetation cover types at Sleeping Bear Dunes National Lakeshore (based on Hazlett 1986).

Forest ecosystem	Area (ha)
Northern Hardwoods	10,276.43
Coastal Forest	4,471.17
Fields	3,181.07
Dunes	1,963.81
Oak-Aspen	1,329.48
Wetlands	303.30
Bluffs	245.41
Conifer Plantation	235.81
Birch-Aspen	207.47
Lake Plain Woods	112.85
Jack Pine	93.30
Black Ash Swamps	65.56
Northern Conifers	44.06
Other	1,428.64
Total	24,063.50

Based on this information, the current landscape of the Lakeshore is dominated by upland northern hardwood forests (42.3%), coastal forests (18.9%) characterized by birch-maple-aspen and oak-pine forest types located in the protected bays along the Lake Michigan shoreline, open fields (13.2%) in varying degrees of succession and ranging from 0.2 ha to 165.5 ha in size, coastal sand dunes (8.3%), and early successional oak-aspen forests (5.6%). Several other cover types are less common across the current Lakeshore landscape, including wetlands (1.3%), bluffs (1.0%), conifer plantations (1.0%), birch-aspen forests (0.9%), lake plain forests (0.5%), jack pine forests (0.4%), black ash swamp forests (0.3%), and northern conifer forests (0.2%) (Table 2).

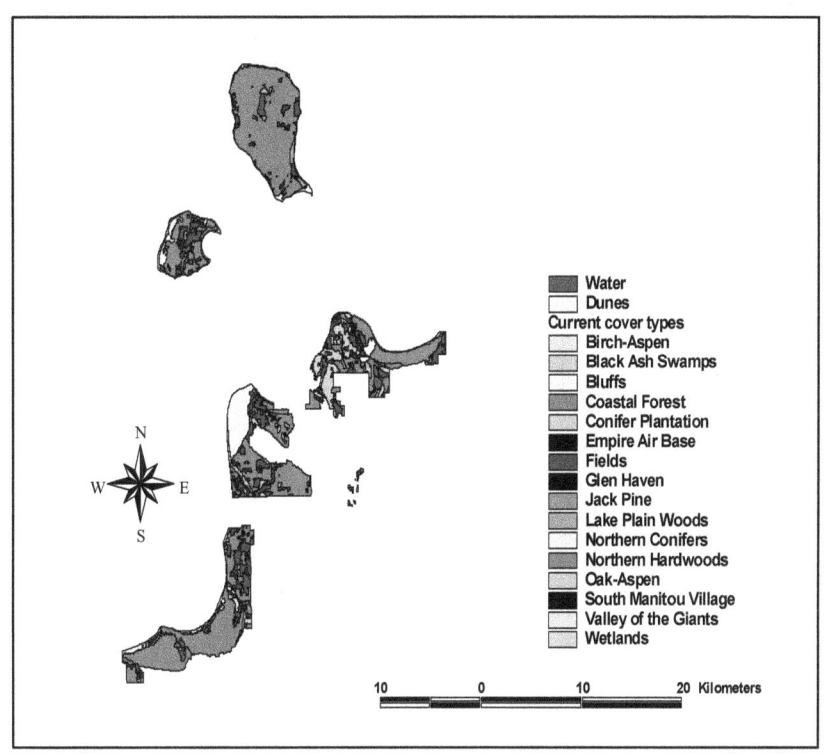

Figure 4. Current vegetation of Sleeping Bear Dunes National Lakeshore (based on Hazlett 1986).

Methods

Distribution and spatial characteristics of openlands

During the summer of 2002, we used a Trimble® Global Positioning System (GPS) unit to geo-reference the boundaries of 12 mainland fields; the Lakeshore's island fields were not studied (Figure 5). While geo-referencing the boundaries of each of these fields, we noted the extent of each field boundary adjacent to the following edge types: developed (includes areas adjacent to roads, houses, barns, etc.), field, forest, or fence line (comprised of old fence rows with various degrees of woody encroachment). Using ArcView® software (Version 3.2), we generated maps of each field and calculated the area (ha), total perimeter (m), area to perimeter ratio (ha:m; lower values indicate a more uniform shape), and the length (m) of each of the four perimeter type categories.

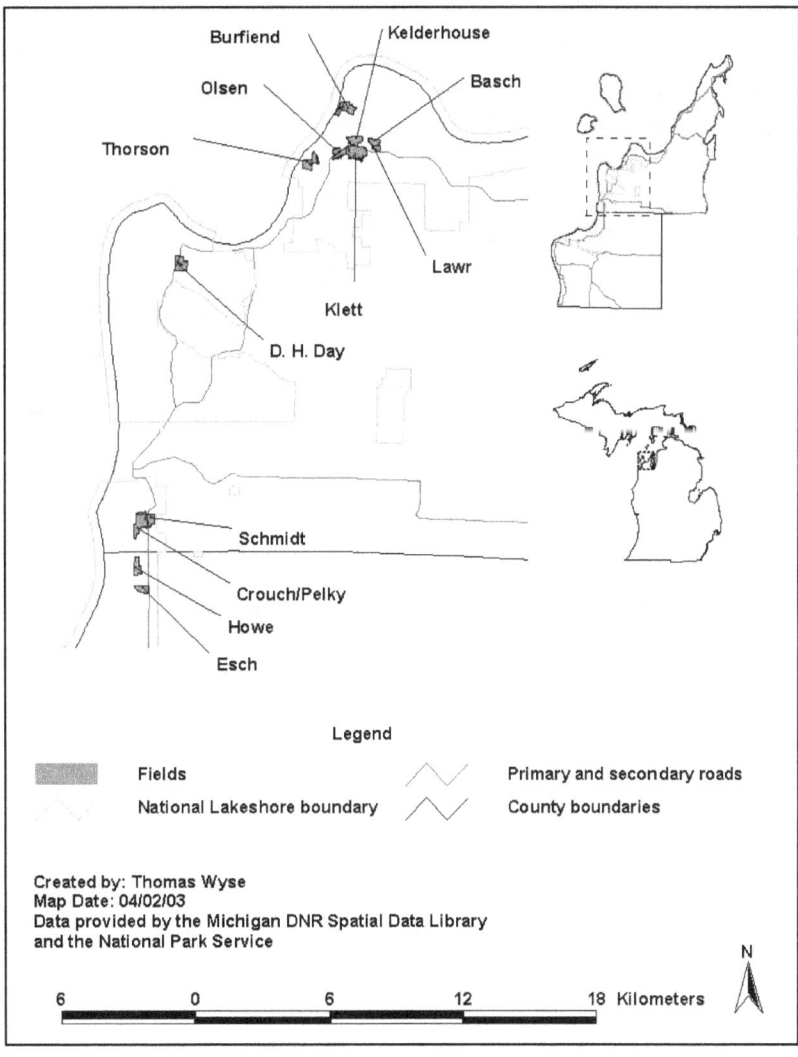

Figure 5. Location of 12 fields of Sleeping Bear Dunes National Lakeshore associated with historic agricultural sites.

9

Vegetation composition and structure of openlands

After geo-referencing the boundaries of the fields, we described the plant communities associated with each field (hereafter referred to as habitat types). In each field, we established three transects (each 30 m in length) associated with each edge type (except for the fence line type which was not present in a majority of the fields studied) and arrayed them perpendicular to the field boundary (Figure 6). Transects were spaced randomly between 20 and 180 m, starting at a random distance 70-180 m from the northwest corner of each of the three edge types. This design was modified when we sampled the small areas associated with the building edge habitat type. In this case, transects were spaced randomly 15 to 25 m apart.

Individual transects included four 100 m^2 sample plots: two located on each side of the field edge at a distance of 5 m and two transects representing the field interior and adjacent boundary type interior (e.g., forest, developed) at a distance of 15 m from the field edge. A total of 215 plots were established across the 12 fields. As the height of the forest canopy was often no more than 10-12 m, we surmised a distance of 15 m was out of the direct influence of the adjacent boundary type and hence represented the field interior from a plant community perspective. Visual walk-through surveys of each field qualitatively supported this assessment. The spatial arrangement of the fields and boundaries dictated how closely we could adhere to these sampling protocols. In some cases, there was not enough space to install three transects per edge type; in others, not all plot centers could be installed. Additionally, many of the adjacent developed areas were not large enough to sample at distances of 15 m from the edge boundary without overlapping with other sample points. Thus, we considered the developed boundary type to be an edge, as the entire area was often within the direct influence of a field edge (hereafter referred to as a "building edge" as all areas sampled were associated with an original homestead) (Figure 6).

In each 100 m^2 plot (radius of 5.64 m), we measured the species and diameter at breast height (DBH) of all woody plants >2.5 cm (Figure 6). We summarized the abundance of woody overstory species by calculating the relative basal area (m^2/ha) of each woody species associated with each habitat type. We examined the relationships among overstory species abundance (using relative basal area as a proxy for abundance) and habitat types using detrended correspondence analysis (DCA). While DCA has been criticized for its use in gradient analyses, in cases where there is a single strong gradient (such as that represented in the current study of forested versus non-forested sites) DCA often performs as well as other techniques such as non-metric, multidimensional scaling (NMS) (McCune and Grace 2002). Additionally, our results suggested that the results DCA provided were interpretable and confirmed patterns in vegetation that we observed among the different habitat types. We supplemented the DCA with Dufrene's and Legendre's (1997) indicator analysis using PC-ORD (McCune and Mefford 1995). These analyses use Monte Carlo permutation procedures to test the association of each species with each habitat type, and they generate a P-value that is the proportion of randomized trials in the permutation procedure with an indicator value equal to or exceeding the observed

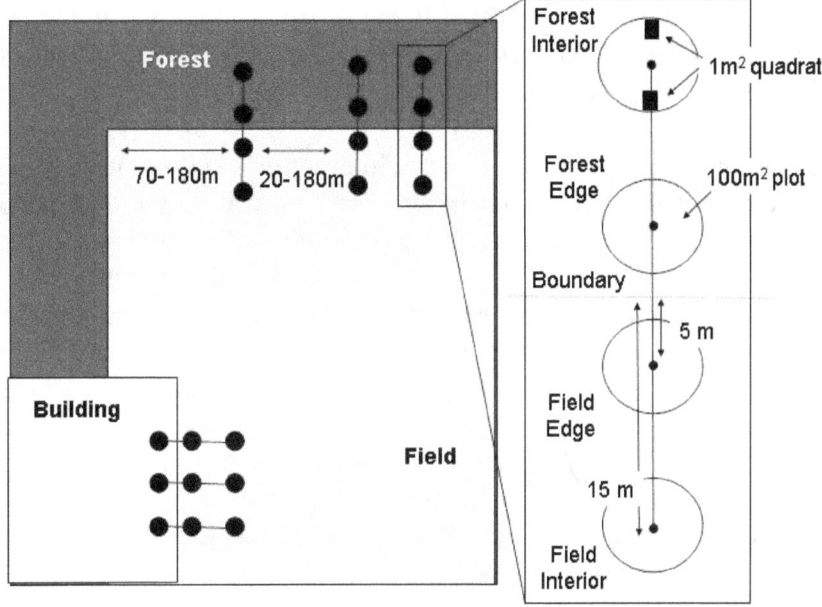

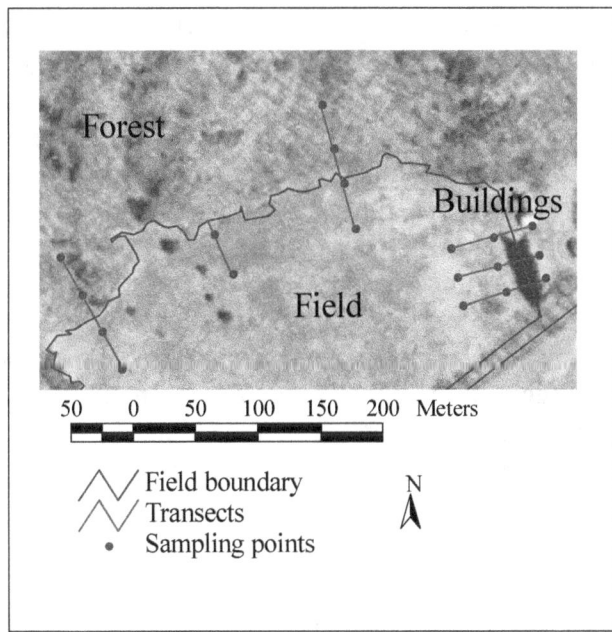

Figure 6. Generalized sampling design used to characterize the vegetation of habitat types associated with openlands at Sleeping Bear Dunes National Lakeshore (top). In some instances this design was modified depending on the characteristics of individual field study areas (see example from the Olsen Farm; bottom).

indicator value (Dufrene and Legendre 1997). Finally, differences in overstory structural characteristics (e.g., overstory species richness, total basal area, and total density) among different habitat types associated with the sampled fields were examined using a one-way analysis of variance (ANOVA). To test for significant differences among habitat types, we used

Tukey's pairwise comparisons (P = 0.05). All data were transformed (arcsin transformation for percentage data) prior to analyses to stabilize variances (Zar 1996).

The ground-flora vegetation (vascular plants <1 m including tree seedlings) was sampled by visually estimating percent-cover of all species in two 1-m^2 quadrats arrayed perpendicular to field boundary, each located 5 m from the plot center (Figure 6). Cover classes included: <1%, 1-5%, 6-10%, 11-20%, 21-40%, 41-70%, and 71-100%. Portions of plants that overhung the plot boundary but were rooted outside of the plot were included in cover estimates. Ground-flora species were grouped into functional life-form guilds (i.e., annual forbs, perennial forbs, graminoids, pteridophytes, woody vines, woody shrubs, and woody seedlings). Nomenclature and life-form categories follow Voss (1972, 1985, 1996), except for pteridophytes (Gleason and Cronquist 1991). Finally, we recorded the percent bare ground present in each 1 m^2 quadrat.

Prior to analyzing the ground-flora vegetation, we substituted the midpoint of each cover class code for the numerical cover class code and then calculated the mean percent-cover for each species and life-form guild. We then examined the distributions of individual species (represented by mean cover values) among different habitat types associated with the historic openlands with DCA using PC-ORD software (McCune and Mefford 1995). As with the overstory analysis, we supplemented the ground-flora ordination with Dufrene's and Legendre's (1997) indicator analysis using PC-ORD (McCune and Mefford 1995). We also used a one-way ANOVA to compare the species richness (total species per m^2), total percent-cover, total percent bare ground, and total percent-cover of each functional life-form guild. We used Tukey's pairwise comparisons to test for significant differences among habitat types (P = 0.05).

Openland bird community assessment

At the Lakeshore scale, we conducted four temporally independent bird surveys to produce a list of all species inhabiting openlands. These surveys also provided a measure of the frequency of registrations/encounters for all species of openland birds. Survey methods were adapted from general recommendations for bird monitoring projects in the Upper Midwest (Howe et al. 1997). We used four-minute roadside point counts at roughly 0.4 km intervals along a 63-stop survey route (Figure 7).

Due to safety concerns and noise, most work was done from either secondary or tertiary roads and some visits required truncating the survey route. Surveys occurred from 0600 to 1200 hr because studies of the song rates for openland birds (unlike species inhabiting forests) show most species sing consistently throughout this time period (Swengel and Swengel 2000). Surveys were not conducted during periods of rain, heavy fog, or high (>24 kph) winds. Data were collected to overlap peak singing times for most species as determined by Brewer et al. (1991). The four visits occurred on: 18 May 2002 (59 point counts), 25 May 2002 (60 point counts), 26 May 2002 (58 point counts), and 9 June 2002 (63 point counts).

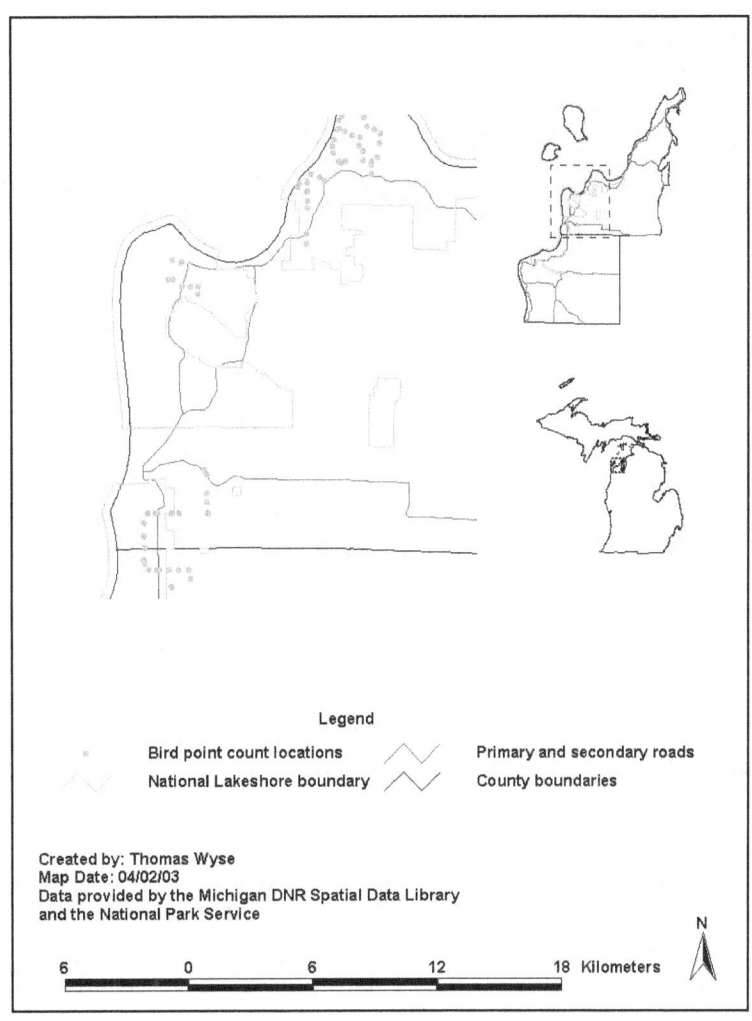

Figure 7. Lakeshore-scale bird survey routes in historic
openland portions of Sleeping Bear Dunes National Lakeshore.

To assess the conservation priority of birds encountered within the openland-dominated portions
of the Lakeshore, we tabulated and compared the national and sub-regional (sub-Upper Midwest)
population trends for all bird species encountered by compiling United States Geological Survey
Breeding Bird Survey (BBS) data from 1966 to 2000 (Sauer et al. 2001). In addition, we used
trend data for BBS Physiographic Stratum 20 (Great Lakes Transition, the stratum in which the
Lakeshore is located), as well as the stratum to the north (Physiographic Stratum 28, Northern
Spruce-Hardwoods) and the two strata in the south combined (Physiographic Stratum 16/17,
Driftless Area and Great Lakes Plain).

Next, we classified species into three broad habitat use categories using Brewer et al. (1991).
Each species was classified as: 1) openland species, 2) grassland species (subset of openland
group), or 3) all others (i.e., forest species, wetland species, etc.). We then pooled only
significant population trend data for the Great Lakes Transition (the BBS physiographic strata
directly associated with the Lakeshore) by habitat use categories to make trend comparisons

between habitat groups using a one-way ANOVA (P = 0.05). The frequency of encountering each species (registration frequency) for all openland species was then used to place species into an ordinal scale of abundance: rare/uncommon, common, and abundant, with each category visually approximated. Finally, to identify priority habitats in the Lakeshore, we used the classification scheme of Brewer et al. (1991) that categorized Michigan birds into 17 preferred breeding habitats. Each species observed in the Lakeshore for which preferred habitats have been identified was grouped into between one and four preferred habitat(s), depending on degree of habitat specificity.

At the field scale, we conducted spot mapping (territory mapping) to assess breeding density of territorial males of grassland bird species in each field. Spot mapping methods followed those discussed in detail by Dickson (1978), Eagles (1981), Verner and Ritter (1988), and Ralph et al. (1993), and were designed for each field using the field maps generated during earlier surveying procedures (see above). Spot mapping is a method by which the position of singing territorial males is marked onto a detailed site map and, when possible, other information helpful in elucidating breeding activity is also recorded (e.g., the presence of a female, aggressive territorial displays toward other males). Each visit to a field requires a fresh map onto which is plotted the position of territorial males encountered during that sampling period.

We made a total of eight visits to each field from mid-May to late June 2002, and after the last survey we created species-specific composite maps for each field. These composites helped us determine the number of individual territories in each field for each species. A minimum of three encounters within a plot was needed for a territory to be considered established. The number of territories was then converted to a 40 ha species-specific density value. One-way ANOVA (P = 0.05) was used to test for differences among the mean densities of each species. To assess the density of species with large area requirements (e.g., upland sandpiper) we used modified spot mapping techniques whereby openlands throughout the mainland portions of the Lakeshore were driven using a vehicle and locations of birds plotted on a Lakeshore-scale map.

We related the densities of openland bird species to characteristics of the fields using canonical correspondence analysis (CCA); CCA is a direct gradient analysis ordination that is constrained by multiple regression of the environmental factors used (ter Braak and Smilauer 1998). Eight factors were used in the CCA, including percent bare ground and the seven field spatial characteristics listed in Table 3.

Results

Distribution and spatial characteristics of openlands

The spatial characteristics of each of the 12 fields examined are listed in Table 3. Mean field size (±1 SE) was 23.6 ha ± 11.2 ha, with the smallest field examined associated with the Lawr Farm (7.2 ha) and the largest fields associated with the Crouch/Pelky (44.2 ha) and Klett (44.4 ha) farms. Most fields had an irregular shape as indicated by the high perimeter-to-area ratios. The areas adjacent to the fields were also somewhat variable, although in most cases between 30% and 67% of the total perimeter length of each field was classified as being developed. The lone exception was the Basch Farm (19% of the field perimeter associated with developed area) which had approximately half of its perimeter adjacent to forest. There were only five fields with fence line borders. When present, this boundary type represented a small proportion of the total length of field boundary.

Table 3. Characteristics of 12 fields at Sleeping Bear Dunes National Lakeshore currently managed as part of the Lakeshore's draft Meadow Management Plan.

| | | | | | Field Perimeter Type | | |
| | | Perimeter | Perimeter | Developed | Field | Forest | Fenceline |
Field Name	Area (ha)	(m)	Area	(m)	(m)	(m)	(m)
Basch	13.2	1,732.7	130.8	335	447	921	-
Burfiend	28.3	4,777.7	160.8	1,844	2,464	-	236
Crouch/Pelky	42.2	4,777.7	113.3	2,470	312	1,719	277
D. H. Day	28.1	3,835.9	136.6	2,242	400	1,194	-
Esch	17.2	1,898.4	110.4	797	-	833	269
Howe	20.8	2,245.0	108.2	949	388	382	528
Kelderhouse	21.3	2,379.2	111.5	1,587	128	664	-
Klett	44.4	4,569.4	103.0	1,519	331	2,486	234
Lawr	7.2	1,233.4	170.8	780	291	162	-
Olsen	20.3	3,886.2	191.8	1,414	371	2,101	-
Schmidt	13.6	1,603.1	118.3	772	492	340	-
Thorson	26.1	3,855.2	147.8	1,705	551	1,599	-
Total	282.7	36,793.9	1,603.3	16,414	6,175	12,401	1,544

Vegetation composition and structure of openlands

Woody species >2.5 cm DBH occurred in approximately 22% of the sample plots (48 of 215 plots). The first axis of the DCA represents a significant gradient of canopy closure ($r = -0.65$, $P = 0.03$), with forest interior and forest edge sample plots on the left side of the ordination and the more open-canopied field edge and field interior sample plots on the right side of the ordination (Figure 8). In those few cases where trees were observed at low densities in the field edge and field interior habitat types, black cherry, often considered an early successional or old-field species, was dominant. The building edge habitat type was dominated by few, large sugar maple stems, while the forest edge and forest interior habitat types were also dominated by sugar maple, but of more varying size. Although not statistically significant, the second DCA axis represents a gradient separating forest habitat types dominated by sugar maple and northern red oak from those dominated by sugar maple, American beech, and eastern hemlock. Corresponding to these differences in community composition, we observed significant differences in species richness of woody plant communities among habitat types (F = 4.51; df = 4; P = 0.004). Specifically, both the forest edge and forest interior habitat types had significantly higher species richness than the other three habitat types (Figure 9).

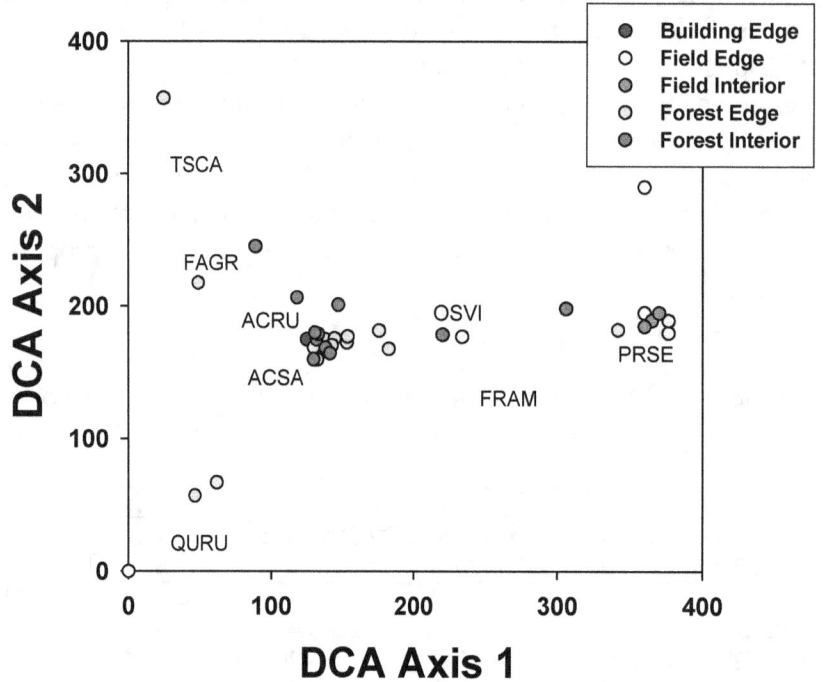

Figure 8. DCA ordination of the overstory of different habitat types associated with the openlands of Sleeping Bear Dunes National Lakeshore. See Appendix B for list of species acronyms; only significant indicator species are included.

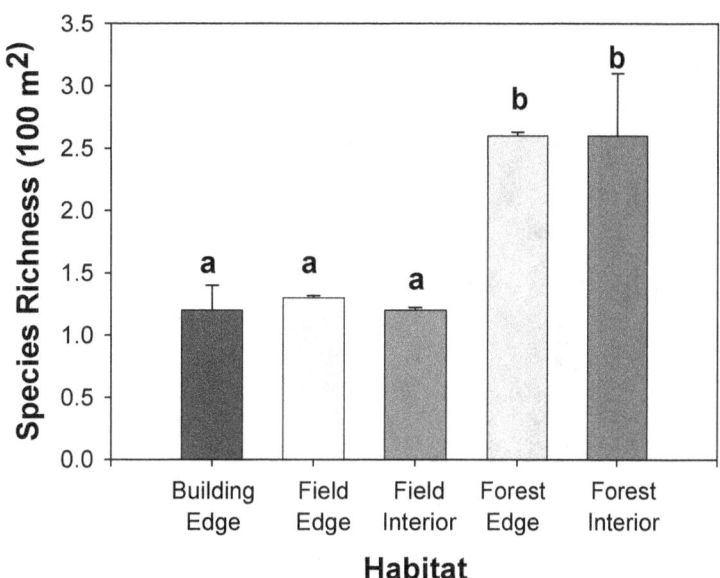

Figure 9. Mean (+/- 1 SE) overstory species richness (100 m^2) by habitat type of openlands of Sleeping Bear Dunes National Lakeshore. Means with different letters indicate a significant difference (P <0.05).

We also observed significant differences among habitat types in terms of total basal area (F = 3.84; df = 4; P = 0.009) and total density (F = 3.43; df = 4; P = 0.016) (Figure 10 and 11, respectively). Total basal area was highest in the building edge habitat type (117.0 + 38.6 m^2/ha), most likely the result of large shade trees that often dominate the original homesteads. However, this value was not significantly higher than the other habitat types, except for the field edge habitat type which had the lowest observed mean basal area (9.9 ± 3.2 m^2/ha). The fact that the field edge habitat had a lower observed basal area is indicative of some large remnant individual trees that occur with the field interior of some of the historic openlands. Total stem density was significantly higher in the forest edge and forest interior habitat types (2,698 ± 598 and 1,964 ± 400 stems/ha, respectively) than the building edge, field edge, and field interior habitat types. The field edge and field interior habitat types were characterized by 543 ± 136 stems/ha and 400 ± 164 stems/ha, respectively (Figure 11). Additionally, the ground-flora DCA (Figure 12) suggests that the ground-flora composition of the field edge, building edge, and field interior habitat types were quite similar to each other, while the composition of the forest edge and forest interior habitat types differed (r = 0.54, P < 0.01). The distribution of sample points and species along the second DCA axis is less clear, but the spread of forest edge and forest interior sample points along the second DCA axis was most likely associated with specific stand histories of the forested areas adjacent to the historic openlands or the different forest types associated with the fields studied (see Figure 8). The specific ground-flora indicator species associated with each habitat type are listed in Figure 12. Although not currently found at high densities in these fields, the invasive and noxious spotted knapweed was present in each field.

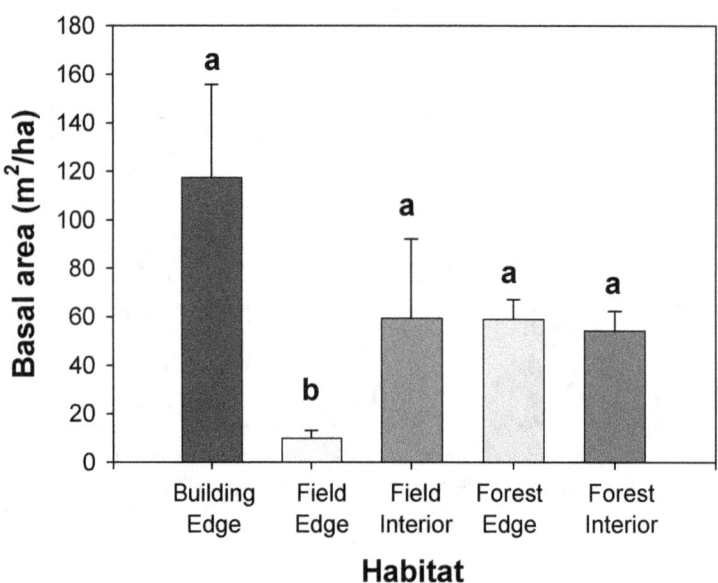

Figure 10. Mean (+/- 1 SE) overstory basal area (m^2/ha) by habitat type of openlands of Sleeping Bear Dunes National Lakeshore. Means with different letters indicate a significant difference (P <0.05).

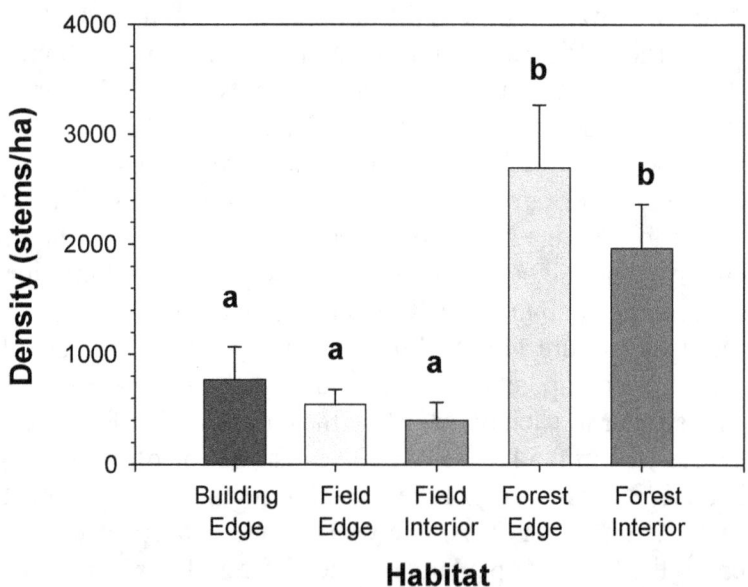

Figure 11. Mean (+/- 1 SE) stem density (stems/ha) by habitat type of openlands of Sleeping Bear Dunes National Lakeshore. Means with different letters indicate a significant difference (P <0.05).

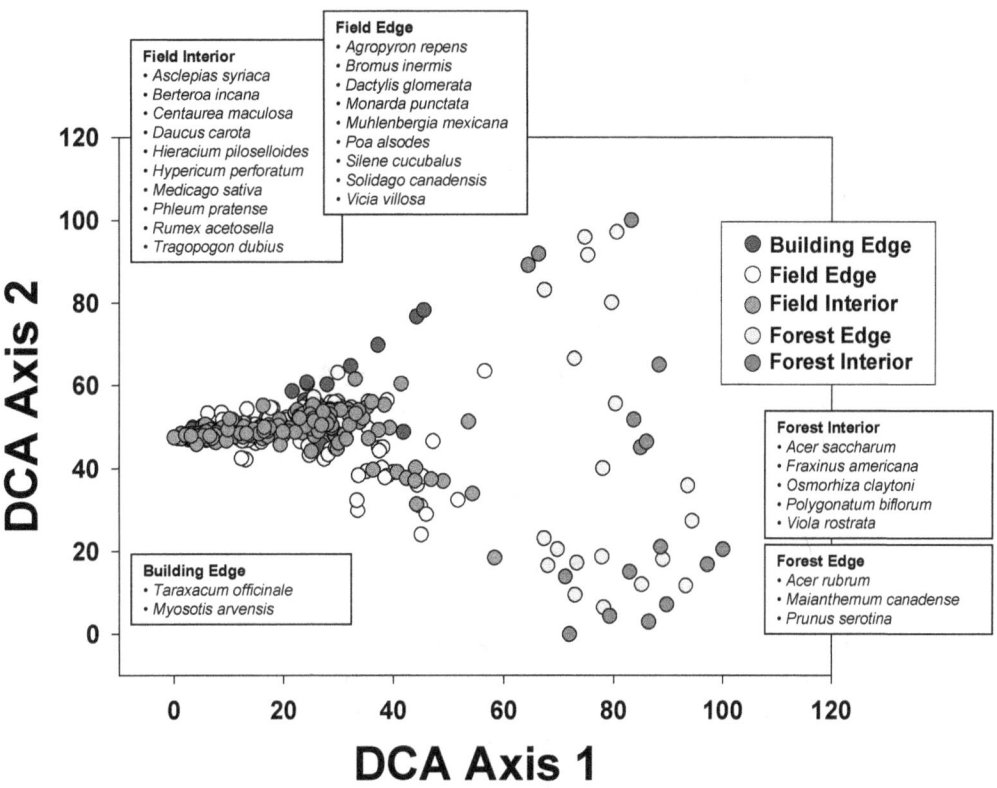

Figure 12. DCA ordination of the ground-flora of different habitat types associated with the openlands of Sleeping Bear Dunes National Lakeshore. Species lists represent the significant indicators associated with each habitat type as determined by the Indicator Analysis.

Corresponding to differences in the ground-flora composition, significant differences were found in species richness (F = 5.78; df = 4; P <0.001) and percent bare ground (F = 35.89; df = 4; P <0.001) among the five different habitat types. The highest mean (±1 SE) ground-flora species richness values per m^2 were found in the field edge (4.8 ± 0.1) and field interior (4.7 ± 0.2) habitat types (Figure 13). The field edge habitat type had significantly higher species richness than the building edge, forest edge, and forest interior habitat types. The field interior habitat type had significantly higher species richness than the building edge and forest edge habitat types. Finally, the cover of bare ground on average was greater than 40% per m^2 in all areas; however bare ground cover was significantly higher in the forest edge and forest interior habitat types than the building edge, field edge, and field interior habitat types (Figure 14).

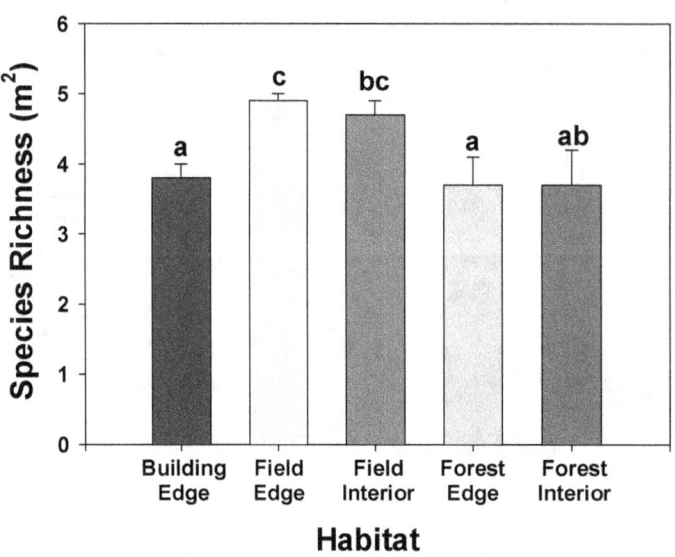

Figure 13. Mean (+/- 1 SE) ground-flora species richness (m^2) by habitat types of openlands of Sleeping Bear Dunes National Lakeshore. Means with different letters indicate a significant difference (P <0.05).

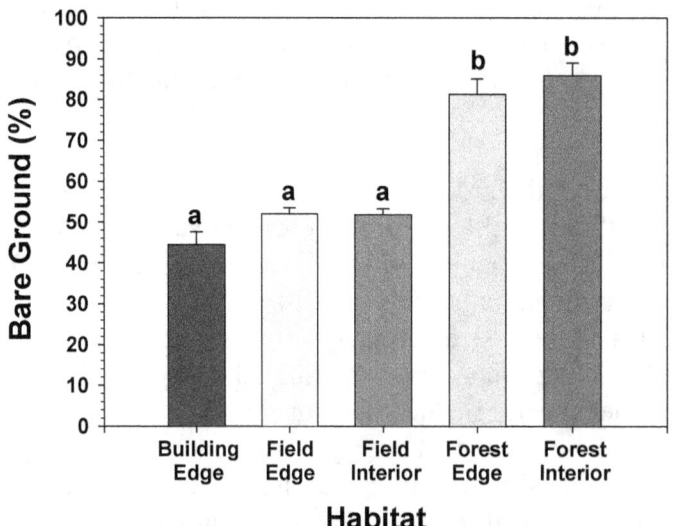

Figure 14. Mean (+/- 1 SE) percent bare ground by habitat types of openlands of Sleeping Bear Dunes National Lakeshore. Means with different letters indicate a significant difference (P <0.05).

We also observed significant differences in the percent-cover of different ground-flora functional life-form guilds among the habitat types examined in this study (Figure 15). Percent forb cover was significantly higher in the field than the field edge, forest edge, or building edge habitat types (F = 22.48; df = 4; P <0.001). Graminoid cover also differed significantly among habitat types (F = 32.10; df = 4; P <0.001), with the highest graminoid cover associated with the building edge habitat. Similarly, graminoid cover in the field edge and field interior habitat types was significantly higher than in either forest habitat type.

As anticipated, tree seedling cover was also significantly different among habitat types (F = 29.31; df = 4; P <0.001), with the cover of seedlings significantly higher in the forest edge habitat types than the building edge, field edge, or field interior habitat types (Figure 15).

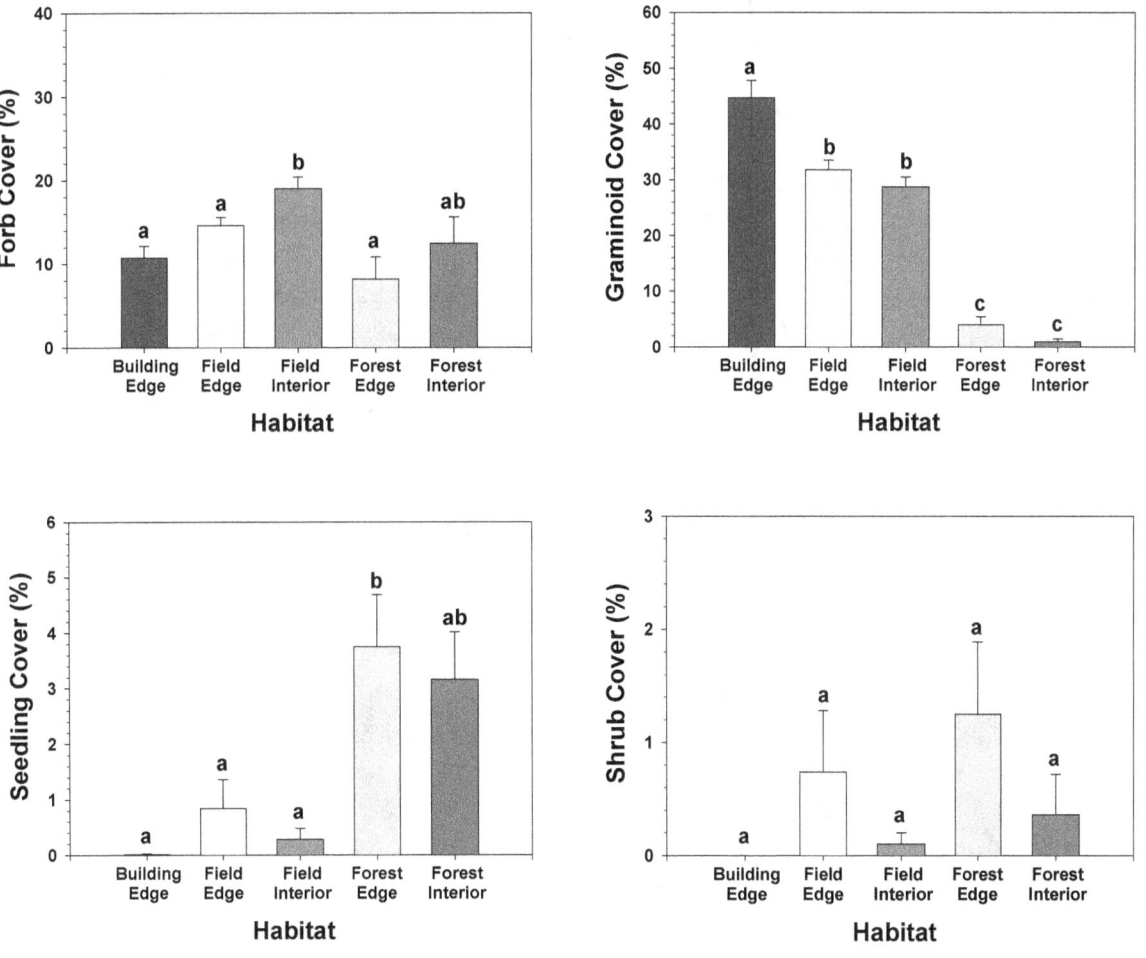

Figure 15. Mean (±1 SE) percent-cover of functional ground-flora life-form guilds by habitat types associated with openlands of Sleeping Bear Dunes National Lakeshore. Comparisons among habitat types were made only for individual life-form categories and means with different letters indicate a significant difference (P <0.05).

No differences were detected in shrub cover among habitat types (Figure 15). However, there was considerable variation observed among shrub cover across all sample plots.

Openland bird community assessment

A total of 83 bird species were encountered at the Lakeshore. See Appendix A for common names, scientific names, and American Ornithologists' Union four-letter species codes. Thirty-six species (43.4%) were classified as openland species, 16 species (19.3%) were classified as grassland bird species, and 31 species (37.3%) were classified as using other habitats. Thirteen openland species observed in the Lakeshore are listed as United States Fish and Wildlife Service Region Three (Midwest) Conservation Priorities: black-billed cuckoo, bobolink, Connecticut warbler, eastern meadowlark, field sparrow, grasshopper sparrow, Henslow's sparrow, Le Conte's sparrow, northern harrier, sedge wren, upland sandpiper, western meadowlark, and whip-poor-will (USFWS 2002). Four other Species of Conservation Priority that utilize other habitats were also observed: black-throated blue warbler, northern flicker, wood duck, and wood thrush. Connecticut warbler, Le Conte's sparrow, and sedge wren are also listed as conservation priorities by Partners in Flight for the Boreal Hardwood Transition zone (an amalgamation of Physiographic Strata 20 and 28) (Partners in Flight 2001).

Breeding Bird Survey population trend data are shown in Appendix C. Of those species for which long-term population data exist survey-wide and sub-regionally, we found that 53% are declining survey-wide, 49% are declining in the Northern Spruce/Hardwoods strata, 50% in the Great Lakes Transition strata, and 36% in the Driftless Area and Great Lakes Plain combined. Forty species had significant population trend data for the Great Lakes Transition Physiographic Stratum. Of these, eight were considered shrubland species, nine were grassland species (i.e., 17 species were classified as openland species), and 23 breed in other habitats. Trend data depict the most severe population declines for the grassland species group, followed by the pooled openland species group. Overall, population trends are increasing for species breeding in other habitats and for all species pooled (Figure 16).

The average (±1 SE) population trend for species breeding in forests (n = 8) was also found to be increasing: 3.38 (±4.76). Population trends for openland birds were not significantly different than trends for species inhabiting other habitats (F = 2.00, df = 1, P >0.05). However, after removing trend data for shrubland species, we found a significant difference in population trends between the grassland bird habitat group and species utilizing non-openland habitats (F = 8.89, df = 1, P = 0.01).

Mean frequency of registration (the mean percentage of stops at which a given species was recorded) for all openland species encountered at least twice during the four visits is shown in Figure 17. Five of the seven species listed as "abundant" were grassland species, compared to four of nine "common" species and two of five species listed as "rare/uncommon." The five most preferred habitats were found to be residential, old field, pasture, shrub upland, and dry deciduous forest. The fewest species were associated with wet coniferous forest (Figure 18).

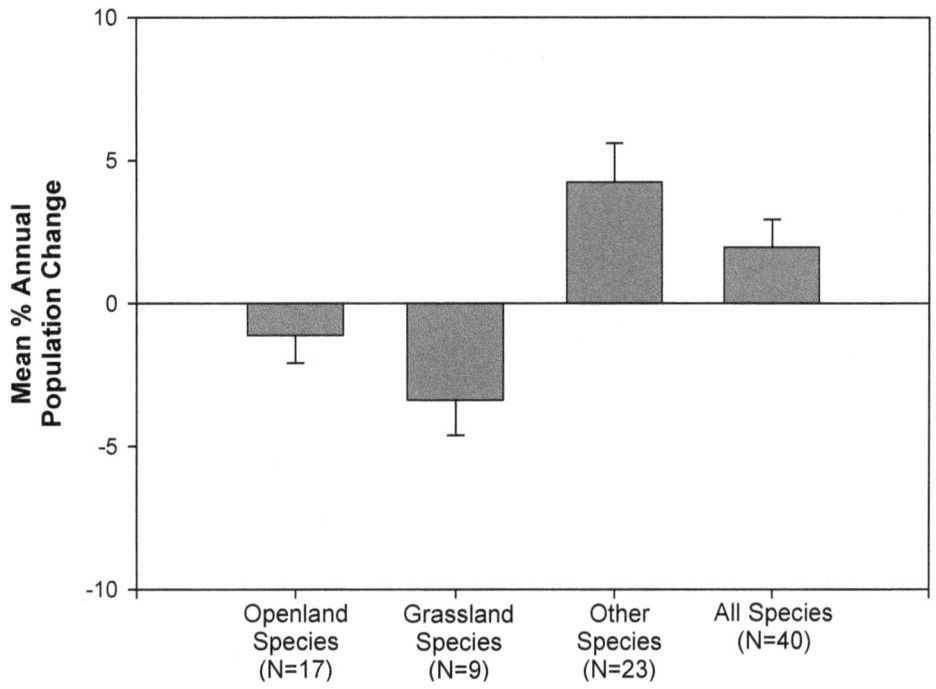

Figure 16. Mean (±1 SE) annual population change by breeding habitat group for those bird species at Sleeping Bear National Lakeshore having significant BBS Great Lakes Transition Physiographic Stratum population trend data (Sauer et al. 2001). The grassland species group is a subset of openland species.

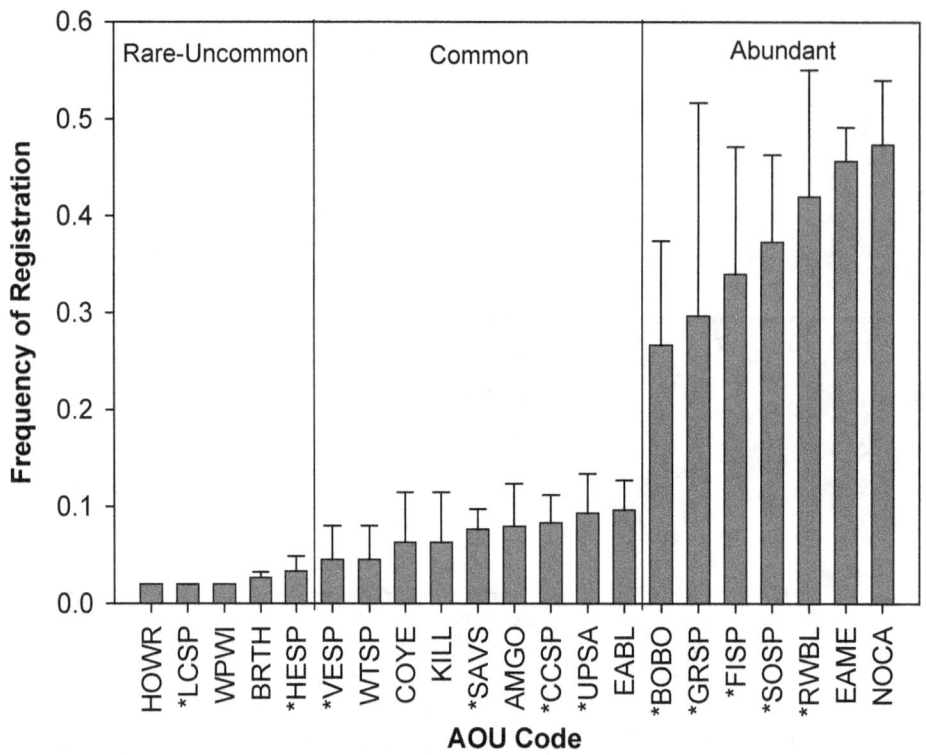

Figure 17. Mean (±1 SE) frequency of registration and ordinal scale of abundance for 21 species of openland birds (* = grassland species) encountered at least twice during four separate landscape-scale surveys within openland portions of Sleeping Bear Dunes National Lakeshore. Species four-letter abbreviations (codes) are those of the American Ornithologists Union, see Appendix A for common and scientific names associated with these codes.

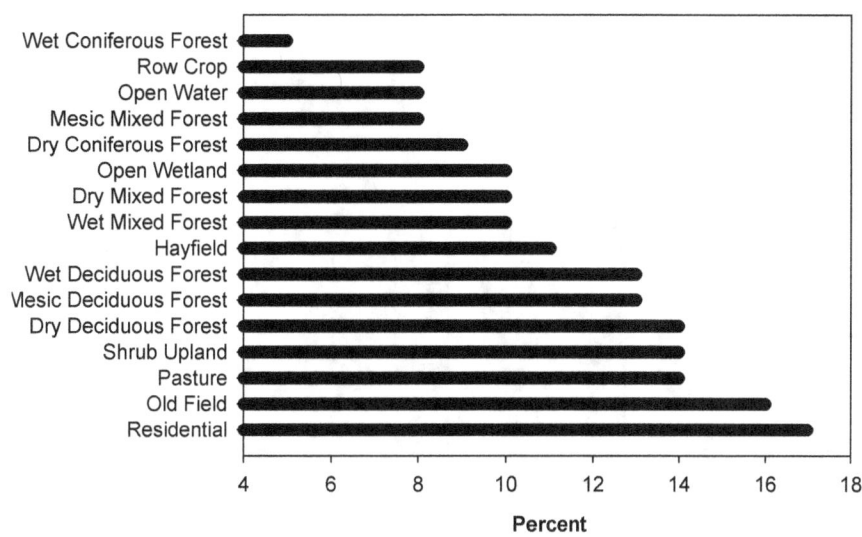

Figure 18. Percent of bird species within historic openland portions of Sleeping Bear Dunes National Lakeshore by preferred habitat(s) in Michigan (from Brewer et al. 1991).

Historic openlands within the Lakeshore are inhabited by bird species considered shortgrass species (e.g., grasshopper sparrow, upland sandpiper, vesper sparrow, western meadowlark), midgrass species (e.g., bobolink, eastern meadowlark, and savannah sparrow), tallgrass species (e.g., Henslow's sparrow, Le Conte's sparrow, sedge wren), and other species requiring some degree of woody vegetation (e.g., clay-colored sparrow and field sparrow) (Sample and Mossman 1997). Of the 16 grassland species observed in the landscape-scale survey, 15 were observed in our study fields. Northern harrier was not registered in any field in which density data were collected. The most ubiquitous species were eastern meadowlark, grasshopper sparrow, red-winged blackbird, and song sparrow; each species was registered in all 12 fields. The other species with registrations in multiple fields (and the number of fields in which they were registered) were: vesper and savannah sparrows (10 fields each), field sparrow (nine), bobolink (eight), upland sandpiper (five), brown-headed cowbird (four), and Le Conte's sparrow (two). Henslow's sparrow, sedge wren, and western meadowlark were each registered only in one field. The number of grassland species in fields ranged from a low of six (D. H. Day) to a high of 11 (Crouch-Pelky). Average (± 1 SE) grassland species richness was 8.4 (1.6) and tended to increase with field size, although no significant relationship was observed ($r^2 = 0.09$, P >0.05). Both the mode and median were nine species. No significant differences were found in the mean densities of bobolink, eastern meadowlark, grasshopper sparrow, red-winged blackbird, and song sparrow (F = 0.61, df = 4, P >0.05) (Figure 19). These values were, however, significantly higher than the mean densities of field sparrow and savannah sparrow (F = 2.99, df = 6, P = 0.01). Moreover, the densities of species were independent of field size (Figure 20). Nine upland sandpiper territories were identified in the Lakeshore.

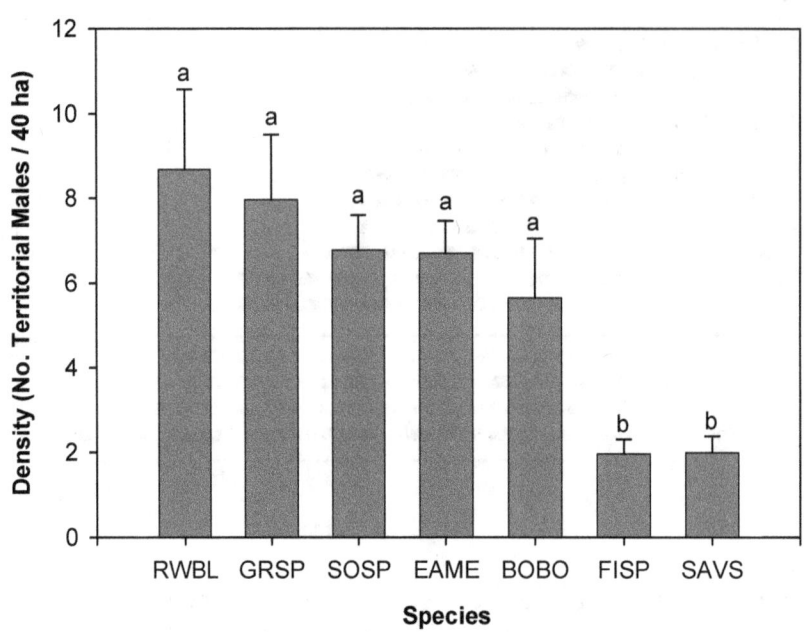

Figure 19. Mean (±1 SE) density of territorial males of seven grassland bird species at Sleeping Bear National Lakeshore. Only data for species with territories in two or more fields are included. Species four-letter abbreviations are those of the American Ornithologists Union. Different letters denote species with significantly different ($P < 0.05$) densities.

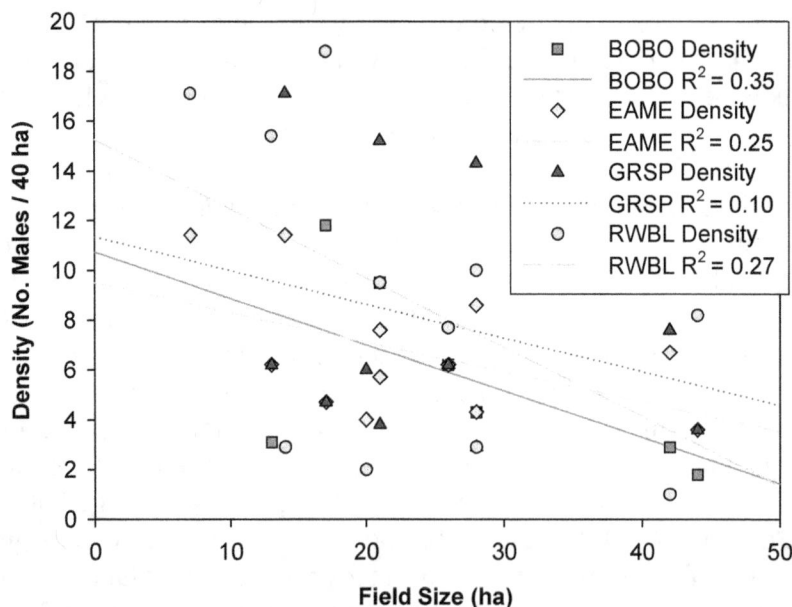

Figure 20. Regression analyses for density of four grassland bird species by field size at Sleeping Bear National Lakeshore. No significant relationships were found ($P > 0.05$). Species four-letter abbreviations are those of the American Ornithologists Union; see Appendix A for common names.

26

Factors regulating the distribution of openland bird species

The results of the CCA reveal that there was no significant relationship between the densities of openland species and field size alone (Figure 21). That is, field size alone did not explain differences in densities of species studied. However, there were significant relationships among densities of openland species and a combination of field size and other field characteristics (combined variance explained by both axes = 65.1%; Axis 1 = 41.3% and Axis 2 = 23.8%). Based on the CCA, the vesper sparrow (VESP), song sparrow (SOSP), and (to a lesser degree) the field sparrow (FISP) tended to be associated with fields with higher percentages of bare ground. Larger fields with higher percentage of field edge were associated with the clay-colored sparrow (CCSP) and grasshopper sparrow (GRSP). Similarly, the CCA suggests that the bobolink (BOBO), savannah sparrow (SAVS), and (to some extent) eastern meadowlark (EAME) also tend to be associated with larger fields that have a higher percentage of fence line perimeter. Finally, some targeted species appear to be ubiquitous. These include the red-winged blackbird (RWBL) and field sparrow (FISP) (Figure 21).

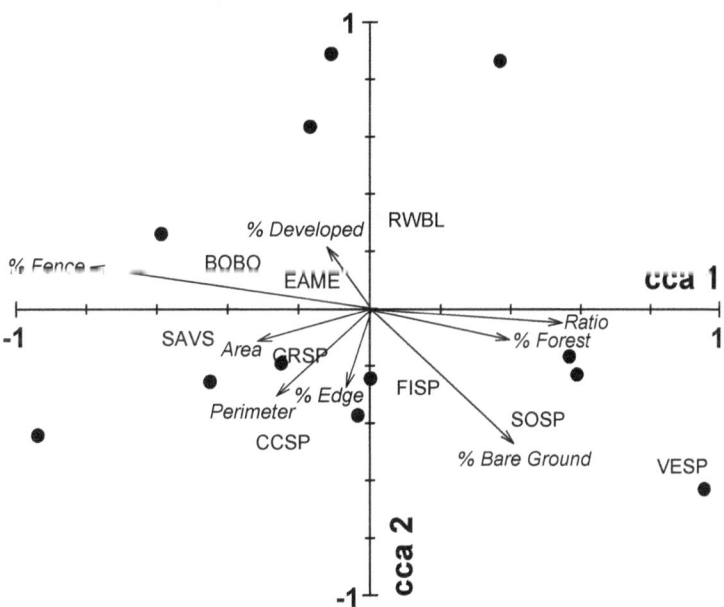

Figure 21. CCA triplot relating openland bird species to spatial characteristics of openlands at Sleeping Bear Dunes National Lakeshore. Solid circles represent individual fields. See Appendix A for bird species acronyms; "Ratio" refers to perimeter-to-area ratio.

Discussion

Throughout North America and the Upper Midwest in particular, the amount of native openland habitat (e.g., prairie, jack pine barrens) has been declining due in part to changes in land use, fire suppression, and active reforestation (Curtis 1959; Niemi and Probst 1990; Askins 2000). Consequently, the conservation of anthropogenic openlands may play an important role in maintaining viable populations of many openland bird species of conservation concern (Sample and Mossman 1997; Askins 2000; Corace 2007; Corace et al. 2009).

As part of a broader assessment of openland birds and their habitats in the Upper Midwest, previous studies have assessed land cover as it relates to openland bird distributions, bird population trends, and habitat affinities and then integrated these findings to assess the effects that hayfield mowing has on bird population trends (Corace 2007; Corace et al. 2009). Results indicated that of all the openland cover in the three Upper Midwest states of Michigan, Minnesota, and Wisconsin, row crops (a habitat of little value for most bird species) represented the dominant cover type, followed by pasture-hayland. In the central portion of the Upper Midwest where the greatest area is devoted to hay production, alfalfa—more intensively managed than mixed grass hay—predominates (Figure 22). Low-intensity managed hayfield habitats (similar to historic openlands of the Lakeshore) were found to be commonly or very commonly used by a number of species discussed in this present study (i.e., bobolink, eastern meadowlark, grasshopper sparrow, savannah sparrow, and western meadowlark). On average, the Upper Midwest represents 20% of the breeding range for each of these species. Moreover, low-intensity managed hayfields (such as those within the Lakeshore) are of even greater importance because mortality to eggs and young by haying machinery is minimal (Bollinger et al. 1990). Together, these findings support the contention of Sample and Mossman (1997) that hayfields represent a habitat type of considerable importance for maintaining local, state-wide, and regional populations of many grassland species.

At the Michigan level, our findings suggest that the community composition of openland birds found within the Lakeshore and identified as conservation priorities by the USFWS differs from the openland bird communities of other landscapes in northern Michigan (Corace 2007). Many of these differences are the result of bird distribution patterns that might be constrained by habitat or other factors. In fact, many of these species of concern have limited distributions within the state (Table 4).

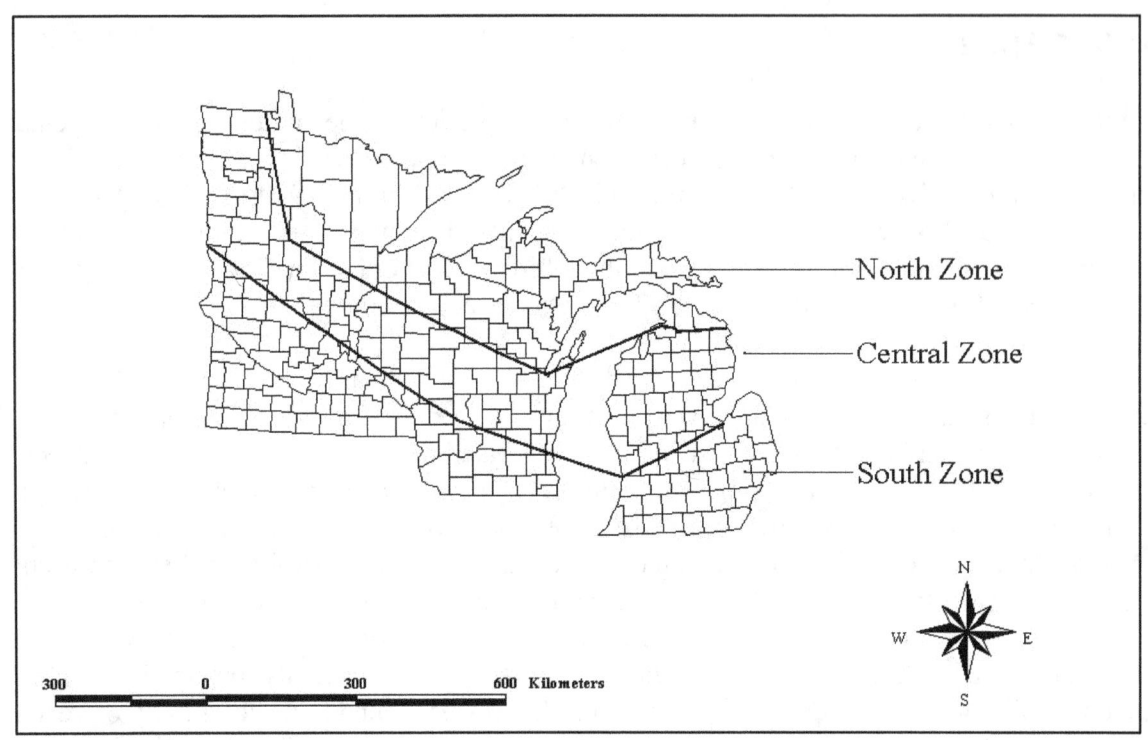

Figure 22. Zones approximating portions of Breeding Bird Survey Physiographic Strata of the Upper Great Lakes region: North Zone = North Spruce / Hardwoods; Central Zone = Great Lakes Transition; South Zone = Driftless Area and Great Lakes Plain (Sauer et al. 2001).

Table 4. Michigan Breeding Bird Atlas block totals[a] (Relative Block Indices) for 13 openland bird species listed as United States Fish and Wildlife Service Region Three (Midwest) Conservation Priorities (Brewer et al. 1991).

Species	Upper Peninsula	Northern Lower Peninsula	Southern Lower Peninsula	Total
Black-billed cuckoo	229 (0.41)	449 (0.53)	540 (0.36)	1,218 (0.42)
Bobolink	287 (0.52)	692 (0.81)	1,333 (0.90)	2,312 (0.80)
Connecticut warbler	58 (0.10)	9 (0.01)	1 (0.00)	68 (0.02)
Eastern meadowlark	195 (0.35)	800 (0.94)	1,820 (1.22)	2,815 (0.97)
Field sparrow	47 (0.08)	784 (0.92)	1,824 (1.23)	2,655 (0.92)
Grasshopper sparrow	34 (0.06)	281 (0.33)	499 (0.34)	814 (0.28)
Henslow's sparrow	18 (0.03)	75 (0.09)	180 (0.12)	273 (0.09)
Le Conte's sparrow	37 (0.07)	0 (0.00)	0 (0.00)	37 (0.01)
Northern harrier	226 (0.41)	230 (0.27)	217 (0.15)	673 (0.23)
Sedge wren	133 (0.24)	128 (0.15)	249 (0.17)	510 (0.18)
Upland sandpiper	95 (0.17)	369 (0.43)	131 (0.09)	595 (0.21)
Western meadowlark	19 (0.03)	60 (0.07)	61 (0.04)	140 (0.05)
Whip-poor-will	151 (0.27)	297 (0.35)	179 (0.12)	627 (0.22)
Average	118 (0.21)	321 (0.38)	541 (0.36)	980 (0.34)

[a]Block totals refer to the number of survey blocks for which a species was found in each of the three survey divisions in Michigan: Upper Peninsula, Northern Lower Peninsula, and Southern Lower Peninsula. Relative Block Indices are used to describe how widespread a species is in the three divisions. Widespread species have values >1.0; species of limited distribution have values approaching zero.

At the field scale, we found that both the vegetation and bird communities varied from field to field. However, the composition of each community seemed to fall in the range of conditions typical of "old field" conditions in the Upper Midwest (Sample and Mossman 1997). Although statistically significant differences in plant species richness between some fields were observed, the ecological significance of this finding is unknown. Vessby et al. (2002) suggested increases in grassland plant species richness may be correlated with increases in diversity of grassland birds (Vessby et al. 2002). We suggest that conditions observed in low-intensity managed fields provide structural diversity and (for most grassland species) improved habitat quality compared to intensively managed hayfields in the Upper Midwest (Corace 2009).

Although grassland bird densities were not positively correlated to field size – a finding similar to that of Ribic and Sample (2001) who studied grassland birds in Wisconsin – larger fields did tend to have a more diverse bird community. Moreover, upland sandpiper (an "area sensitive" species) was only observed in Basch, Crouch/Pelky, Howe, Kelderhous, Klett, and Schmidt. We believe this species was only observed in these fields because of their proximity to each other and thus the formation of larger habitat units: Crouch/Pelky-Howe-Schmidt (total 76.6 ha) and Basch-Kelderhouse-Klett (total 78.9 ha). Additionally, our multivariate analyses suggest that the density of openland species may be regulated by the interaction of field size, shape, and edge type. Many species (e.g., bobolink, clay-colored sparrow, grasshopper sparrow, and savannah sparrow) tended to be associated with fields with limited barriers (e.g., fencelines, roads), further suggesting that the interconnectivity of individual fields is an important characteristic of the Lakeshore landscape. Similar results have been published by Helzer and Jelinski (1999) who found patch area and perimeter-area ratio a strong predictor of species presence and richness in a study of wet meadow grasslands in Nebraska.

Future research should address to what degree maintaining historic openland communities within the Lakeshore influences other wildlife species, including forest birds. Both brood parasitism and nest predation are known to be considerable influences on bird productivity (Heske et al. 2001). We found relatively few brown-headed cowbirds in our work and those birds observed seemed to be associated with maintained lawns around historic farmhouses and other buildings. Bayne and Hobson (1997) suggest that differences in bird predator communities exist between agriculturally-fragmented forested landscapes, and other authors have suggested that predation by small mammals may be underestimated (Heske et al. 2001). However, more work is required to assess the meso-mammal community of the Lakeshore and place these findings into the context of historic openland conservation.

Coupled with the broader context of habitat availability and distribution patterns, our findings suggest historic openlands of the Lakeshore represent an area of considerable conservation value at multiple scales. Furthermore, the fact that the majority of historic openlands occur on the most common and best represented ecosystem type at the Lakeshore (sites where the reference condition is a beech-sugar maple-hemlock forest ecosystem) suggests that the maintenance of these landscapes as openlands may not have a dramatic influence on the conservation status of this ecosystem when compared with other more rare ecosystems at the Lakeshore (for more information see: http://snr.osu.edu/research/goebel/web/slbe-ref.htm).

Recommendations for maintaining openland bird communities

If the goal of openland management at the Lakeshore is to conserve openland bird diversity, management must consider habitat variables spatially and temporally at both the landscape and field scales. Spatially, our results suggest that, in conjunction with other variables, field size is an important factor. In particular, many of the grassland species found at the Lakeshore are considered area-sensitive (Swanson 1998; Dechant et al. 1999a, 1999b, 1999c; Hull 2000; Dechant et al. 2001). That is, for a number of species (e.g., bobolink, eastern meadowlark, grasshopper sparrow, Henslow's sparrow, northern harrier, savannah sparrow, sedge wren, vesper sparrow, and upland sandpiper), the size and connectivity of habitat patches may influence either species presence, abundance, or density. Consequently, management should focus on the proximity and size of management units and should promote or maintain larger management areas (i.e., specific habitat unit [or field] plus surrounding suitable habitat). By maintaining a high degree of connectivity between fields, management can approach the minimum suggested size of 100 ha openland management areas (Sample and Mossman 1997). The Basch-Kelderhouse-Klett-Olsen and Crouch/Pelky-Esch-Howe-Schmidt field complexes provide examples of such management areas. Not surprisingly, these areas were the only ones in which upland sandpipers were found. Fields isolated from other openland patches (e.g., D. H. Day) could be maintained in early forest successional stages and thus provide habitat for shrubland species that tend to be less sensitive to habitat area size. We also suggest that smaller fields (e.g., Lawr) located within ecosystem types other than the Herb Poor Moraine (HPM) either be restored to a more natural condition or allowed to develop along current successional trajectories.

Within management areas, it is usually best to keep woody vegetation to <5% of the habitat unit; habitat units unsuitable for most grassland birds have >30% woody cover (Sample and Mossman 1997). In our study, 22% of our sample plots had woody vegetation >2.5 cm DBH. Woody vegetation that remains within a unit should consist primarily of shrubs, but a few taller (>3 m) trees could be interspersed. The shape of management areas should be either circular or square to reduce edge effects and provide more interior openland habitat. Suitable surrounding areas should be less linear and may consist of shrubs and other non-grassland habitats; abrupt forest edges adjacent to suitable habitat areas should be avoided

Temporally, management should strive to promote mostly old field conditions of sparse vegetation and a forb-grass mix by providing a disturbance regime at a rate no greater than once every three-to-five years (Sample and Mossman 1997). Prescribed fire and mowing should both be considered (Swanson 1998; Dechant et al. 1999a, 1999b, 1999c; Hull 2000; Dechant et al. 2001). Although grazing by domestic animals can produce desired habitat conditions, this form of management is not recommended because it may lead to increased numbers of associated brown-headed cowbirds. Regardless of disturbance type, managers should rotate disturbance through a management unit so that approximately two-thirds of the unit is treated at a time. This will promote greater vegetative diversity and structure within an area and, thus, increase habitat diversity within management units. Management should occur after the breeding season; a general rule of thumb is to treat areas during the last week in July through August. However, it may become increasingly desirable to reduce spotted knapweed coverage in fields. Mowing while the plant is in bloom to minimize seed production is a possible management strategy (Emery et al. 2003).

Literature Cited

Albert, D. A. 1995. Regional landscape ecosystems of Michigan, Minnesota and Wisconsin: A working map and classification. USDA Forest Service General Technical Report NC-178. North Central Research Station, St. Paul, MN.

Allen, C. D., D. A. Falk, M. Hoffman, J. Klingel, P. Morgan, M. Savage, T. Schulke, P. Stacey, K. Suckling, and T. W. Swetnam. 2002. Ecological restoration of southwestern ponderosa pine ecosystems: A broad framework. Ecological Applications 12:1418-1433.

Askins, R. A. 2000. Restoring North America's Birds: Lessons from Landscape Ecology. Yale University Press, New Haven, CT.

Bayne, E. M., and K. A. Hobson. 1997. Comparing the effects of landscape fragmentation by forestry and agriculture on predation of artificial nests. Conservation Biology 11:1418-1429.

Bollinger, E. K., P. B. Bollinger, and T. A. Gavin. 1990. Effects of hay-cropping on eastern populations of the bobolink. Wildlife Society Bulletin 18:142-150.

Brewer, R., G. A. McPeek, and R. J. Adams. 1991. The Atlas of Breeding Birds of Michigan. Michigan State University Press, Lansing.

Corace, III, R. G. 2007. Using multiple spatial scales to prioritize openland bird conservation in the Midwest. Dissertation. Michigan Technological University, Houghton.

Corace, III, R. G., D. J. Flaspohler, and L. M. Shartell. In Press. Geographic patterns in openland cover and hayfield mowing in the Upper Great Lakes region: Implications for grassland bird conservation. Landscape Ecology.

Curtis, J. T. 1959. The Vegetation of Wisconsin. University of Wisconsin Press, Madison.

Dechant, J. A., M. L. Sondreal, D. H. Johnson, L. D. Igl, C. M. Goldad, M. P. Nenneman, and B. R. Euliss. 1999a. Effects of management on grassland birds: Grasshopper sparrow. Northern Prairie Wildlife Research Center, Jamestown, ND.

Dechant, J. A., M. F. Dinkins, D. H. Johnson, L. D. Igl, C. M. Goldad, B. D. Parkin, and B. R. Euliss. 1999b. Effects of management on grassland birds: Upland sandpiper. Northern Prairie Wildlife Research Center, Jamestown, ND.

Dechant, J. A., M. L. Sondreal, D. H. Johnson, L. D. Igl, C. M. Goldad, A. L. Zimmerman, and B. R. Euliss. 1999c. Effects of management on grassland birds: Bobolink. Northern Prairie Wildlife Research Center, Jamestown, ND.

Dechant, J. A., M. L. Sondreal, D. H. Johnson, L. D. Igl, C. M. Goldade, B. Parkin, and B. R. Euliss. 2001. Effects of management on grassland birds: Field sparrow. Northern Prairie Wildlife Research Center, Jamestown, ND.

Dickson, J. D. 1978. Comparison of breeding bird census techniques. American Birds **32**:10-13.

Dufrene, M., and P. Legendre. 1997. Species assemblages and indicator species: The need for a flexible asymmetrical approach. Ecological Monographs **67**:345-366.

Eagles, P. F. J. 1981. Breeding bird censuses using spot mapping techniques upon samples of homogeneous habitats. Studies in Avian Biology **6**:455-460.

Emery, S. M., K. L. Gross, and K. N. Suding. 2003. Summer burns best for controlling spotted knapweed in prairie restoration experiment (Michigan). Ecological Restoration **21**:137.

Gleason, H. A., and A. Cronquist. 1991. Manual of Vascular Plants of Northeastern United States and Adjacent Canada. New York Botanical Garden, New York.

Hazlett, B. T. 1986. The terrestrial vegetation and flora of the mainland portion of Sleeping Bear Dunes National Lakeshore, Benzie and Leelanau Counties, Michigan. Technical Report No. 13, University of Michigan Biological Station, Douglas Lake, MI.

Helzer, C. J., and D. E. Jelinski. 1999. The relative importance of patch area and perimeter-area ratio to grassland birds. Ecological Applications **9**:1448-1458.

Heske, E. J., S. K. Robinson, and J. D. Brawn. 2001. Nest predation and neotropical songbirds: Piecing together the fragments. Wildlife Society Bulletin **29**:52-61.

Howe, R. W., G. J. Niemi, S. J. Lewis, and D. A. Welsh. 1997. A standard method for monitoring songbird populations in the Great Lakes region. Passenger Pigeon **59**:183–194.

Hull, S. D. 2000. Effects of management practices on grassland birds: Eastern meadowlark. Northern Prairie Wildlife Research Center, Jamestown, ND.

Karamanski, T. J. 2000. A Nationalized Lakeshore: The Creation and Administration of Sleeping Bear Dunes National Lakeshore. National Park Service, U.S. Department of the Interior, Washington, D.C.

Landres, P. B., P. Morgan, and F. J. Swanson. 1999. Overview of the use of natural variability concepts in managing ecological systems. Ecological Applications **9**:1179-1188.

McCune, B., and M. J. Mefford. 1995. PC-ORD. Multivariate analysis of ecological data. Version 2.0. MJM Software Design, Gleneden Beach, OR.

McCune, B., and J. B. Grace. 2002. Analysis of Ecological Communities. MJM Software, Gleneden Beach, OR.

Michigan Department of Natural Resources. 1999. Michigan's Special Animals. Michigan DNR Endangered Species Program and the Michigan Natural Features Inventory, Lansing.

Moore, M. M., W. W. Covington, and P. Z. Fule. 1999. Reference conditions and ecological restoration: A southwestern ponderosa pine perspective. Ecological Applications 9:1266-1277.

National Park Service. 2001. National Park Service Strategic Plan. FY2001-2005. U.S. Department of the Interior, Washington, D.C.

Niemi, G. J., and J. R. Probst. 1990. Wildlife and fire in the upper Midwest. Pages 31-46 *in* J. M. Sweeney, editor. Management of dynamic ecosystems. The Wildlife Society, Lafayette, IN.

Partners in Flight. 2001. Boreal Hardwood Transition priority bird populations and habitats. Online. (https://www.blm/gov/wildlife/pl_20sum.htm).

Ralph, C. J., G. R. Geupel, P. Pyle, T. E. Martin, and D. F. DeSante. 1993. Handbook of field methods for monitoring landbirds. General Technical Report GTR PSW–144. USDA Forest Service, Pacific Southwest Research Station, Albany, CA.

Ribic, C. A., and D. W. Sample. 2001. Associations of grassland birds with landscape factors in southern Wisconsin. American Midland Naturalist 146:105-121.

Sample, D. W., and M. J. Mossman. 1997. Managing Habitat for Grassland Birds: A Guide for Wisconsin. Wisconsin Department of Natural Resources PUBL-SS-925-97. Bureau of Integrated Science Services, Madison.

Sauer, J. R., J. E. Hines, and J. Fallon. 2001. The North American Breeding Bird Survey, Results and Analysis 1966-2000. Version 2001.2. U. S. Geological Survey, Patuxent Wildlife Research Center, Laurel, Maryland.

Scharf, W. C. 1997. Grassland birds and habitat management in Leelanau County, Michigan. Michigan Birds and Natural History 4:133-141.

Sleeping Bear Dunes National Lakeshore. In review. Meadow ecosystem plan. Sleeping Bear Dunes National Lakeshore, Empire, MI.

Swanson, D. A. 1998. Effects of management on grassland birds: Savannah sparrow. Northern Prairie Wildlife Research Center, Jamestown, ND.

Swengel, S. R., and A. B. Swengel. 2000. Influences of seasonal and daily timing on detection of grassland birds. Passenger Pigeon 62:225-237.

ter Braak, C. J. F., and P. Smilauer. 1998. CANOCO reference manual and user's guide to Canoco for Windows: Software for canonical community ordination (Version 4.0). Microcomputer Power, Ithaca, NY.

Thompson, P. W. 1967. Vegetation and Common Plants of Sleeping Bear. Cranbrook Institute of Science Bulletin 52. Bloomfield Hills, MI.

United States Fish and Wildlife Service. 2002. Fish and wildlife resource conservation priorities: Region 3. Minneapolis, MN.

Verner, J., and L. V. Ritter. 1988. A comparison of transects and spot mapping in oak-pine woodlands of California. Condor **90**:401-419.

Vessby, K., B. Söderström, A. Glimskär, and B. Svensson. 2002. Species-richness correlations of six different taxa in Swedish seminatural grasslands. Conservation Biology **16**:430-439.

Voss, E. G. 1972. Michigan Flora. Part I. Gymnosperms and Monocots. Cranbrook Institute of Science, Bloomfield Hills, MI.

Voss, E. G. 1985. Michigan Flora. Part II. Dicots (Saururaceae – Cornaceae). Cranbrook Institute of Science, Bloomfield Hills, MI.

Voss, E. G. 1996. Michigan Flora. Part III. Dicots (Pyrolaceae - Compositae). Cranbrook Institute of Science, Bloomfield Hills, MI.

Zar, J. H. 1996. Biostatistical Analysis, 3rd edition. Prentice-Hall, Inc., Upper Saddle River, NJ.

Appendix A. List of Bird Species

Eighty-three species of birds encountered within historic openland portions of Sleeping Bear Dunes National Lakeshore. Common names in bold denote openland species; common names in italics denote grassland species; *denote Fish and Wildlife Service Region 3 (Midwest) Species of Conservation Priority. Species are listed alphabetically by American Ornithologists' Union (AOU) four-letter code.

AOU Code	Species Name	Common Name
AMCR	*Corvus brachyrhynchos*	American crow
AMGO	***Carduelis tristis***	**American goldfinch**
AMKE	***Falco sparverius***	**American kestrel**
AMRO	*Turdus migratorius*	American robin
BAOR	*Icterus galbula*	Baltimore oriole
BARS	*Hirundo rustica*	Barn swallow
BBCU*	***Coccyzus erythrophthalmus***	**Black-billed cuckoo**
BCCH	*Poecile atricapillus*	Black-capped chickadee
BHCO	***Molothrus ater***	***Brown-headed cowbird***
BLJA	*Cyanocitta cristata*	Blue jay
BOBO*	***Dolichonyx oryzivorus***	***Bobolink***
BRTH	***Toxostoma rufum***	**Brown thrasher**
BTBW*	*Dendroica caerulescens*	Black-throated blue warbler
BTNW	*Dendroica virens*	Black-throated green warbler
BWTE	*Anas discors*	Blue-winged teal
CAGO	*Branta canadensis*	Canada goose
CAWR	*Thryothorus ludovicianus*	Carolina wren
CCSP	***Spizella pallida***	***Clay-colored sparrow***
CEDW	*Bombycilla cedrorum*	Cedar waxwing
CHSP	*Spizella passerine*	Chipping sparrow
COGR	*Quiscalus quiscula*	Common grackle
COHA	*Accipiter cooperii*	Cooper's hawk
CONW*	***Oporornis agilis***	**Connecticut warbler**
CORA	*Corvus corax*	Common raven
COSN	***Gallinago gallinago***	**Common snipe**
COYE	***Geothlypis trichas***	**Common yellowthroat**
CSWA	***Dendroica pensylvanica***	**Chestnut-sided warbler**
DCCO	*Phalacrocorax auritus*	Double-crested cormorant
EABL	***Sialia sialis***	**Eastern bluebird**
EAKI	***Tyrannus tyrannus***	**Eastern kingbird**
EAME*	***Sturnella magna***	***Eastern meadowlark***
EAPH	*Sayornis phoebe*	Eastern phoebe
EATO	***Pipilo erythrophthalmus***	**Eastern towhee**
EUST	*Sturnus vulgaris*	European starling
FISP*	***Spizella pusilla***	***Field sparrow***
GBHE	*Ardea herodias*	Great blue heron
GCFL	*Myarchus crinitus*	Great crested flycatcher
GRCA	***Dumetella carolinensis***	**Gray catbird**
GRHE	*Butorides striatus*	Green heron
GRSP*	***Ammodramus savannarum***	***Grasshopper sparrow***
HAWO	*Picoides villosus*	Hairy woodpecker
HESP*	***Ammodramus henslowii***	***Henslow's sparrow***

Appendix A. List of Bird Species (continued).

AOU Code	Species Name	Common Name
HOFI	*Carpodacus mexicanus*	House finch
HOWR	***Troglodytes aedon***	**House wren**
INBU	***Passerina cyanea***	**Indigo bunting**
KILL	***Charadrius vociferous***	**Killdeer**
LCSP*	***Ammodramus leconteii***	***Le Conte's sparrow***
MALL	*Anas platyrhynchos*	Mallard
MAWA	*Dendroica magnolia*	Magnolia warbler
MODO	*Zenaida macroura*	Mourning dove
NOCA	***Cardinalis cardinalis***	**Northern cardinal**
NOFL*	*Colaptes auratus*	Northern flicker
NOHA*	***Circus cyaneus***	***Northern harrier***
OVEN	*Seiurus aurocapillus*	Ovenbird
PIWO	*Dryocopus pileatus*	Pileated woodpecker
RBGR	*Pheucticus ludovicianus*	Rose-breasted grosbeak
REVI	*Vireo olivaceus*	Red-eyed vireo
RHWO	*Melanerpes erythrocephalus*	Red-headed woodpecker
RTHA	*Buteo jamaicensis*	Red-tailed hawk
RTHU	*Archilochus colubris*	Ruby-throated hummingbird
RUGR	*Bonasa umbellus*	Ruffed grouse
RWBL	***Agelaius phoeniceus***	***Red-winged blackbird***
SAVS	***Passerculus sandwichensis***	***Savannah sparrow***
SCTA	*Piranga olivacea*	Scarlet tanager
SEWR*	***Cistothorus platensis***	***Sedge wren***
SORA	*Porzana carolina*	Sora
SOSP	***Melospiza melodia***	***Song sparrow***
SWSP	*Melospiza georgiana*	Swamp sparrow
TRES	*Tachycineta bicolor*	Tree swallow
TUVU	*Cathartes aura*	Turkey vulture
UPSA*	***Bartramia longicauda***	***Upland sandpiper***
VESP	***Pooecetes gramineus***	***Vesper sparrow***
WBNU	*Sitta carolinensis*	White-breasted nuthatch
WCSP	*Zonotrichia leucophrys*	White-crowned sparrow
WEME	***Sturnella neglecta***	***Western meadowlark***
WPWI	***Caprimulgus vociferus***	**Whip-poor-will**
WITU	*Meleagris gallopavo*	Wild turkey
WODU	*Aix sponsa*	Wood duck
WOTH	*Hylocichla mustelina*	Wood thrush
WTSP	***Zonotrichia albicollis***	**White-throated sparrow**
YBSA	*Syphyrapicus varius*	Yellow-bellied sapsucker
YPWA	***Dendroica palmarum hypochrysea***	**Yellow palm warbler**
YWAR	***Dendroica petechia***	**Yellow warbler**

Appendix B. List of Plant Species

List of plant species (with species codes) sampled in historic openlands and adjacent habitat types (building edge, field edge, field interior, forest edge, forest interior) of Sleeping Bear Dunes National Lakeshore.

Species Name	Code	Species Name	Code	Species Name	Code
Achillea millefolium	ACMI	*Lathyrus sylvestris*	LASY	*Saponaria officinalis*	SAOF
Acer rubrum	ACRU	*Leucanthemum vulgare*	LEVU	*Silene cucubalus*	SICU
Acer saccharum	ACSA	*Lithospermum caroliniense*	LICA	*Silene pratensis*	SIPR
Acer spicatum	ACSP	*Lonicera* sp.	LOxx	*Solidago canadensis*	SOCA
Agropyron repens	AGRE	*Lycopodium clavatum*	LYCL	*Tsuga canadensis*	TSCA
Amaranthus retroflexus	AMRE	*Maianthemum canadense*	MACA	*Tragopogon dubius*	TRDU
Amelanchier sp.	AMxx	*Malva neglecta*	MANE	*Ulmus americana*	ULAM
Antennaria parlinii	ANNE	*Malus* sp.	Maxx		
Aquilegia canadensis	AQCA	*Medicago lupulina*	MELU		
Arctium minus	ARMI	*Medicago sativa*	MESA		
Arenaria serpyllifolia	ARSE	*Milium effusum*	MIEF		
Arisaema triphyllum	ARTR	*Mitchella repens*	MIRE		
Asclepias syriaca	ASSY	*Monarda punctata*	MOPU		
Berteroa incana	BEIN	*Muhlenbergia mexicana*	MUME		
Betula papyrifera	BEPA	*Myosotis arvensis*	MYAR		
Berberis thunbergii	BETH	*Osmorhiza claytoni*	OSCL		
Carex sp.	CAxx	*Ostrya virginiana*	OSVI		
Cerastium fontanum	CEFO	*Panicum praecocius*	PAPR		
Centaurea maculosa	CEMA	*Physalis heterophylla*	PHHE		
Circaea alpine	CIAL	*Phleum pretense*	PHPR		
Cirsium vulgare	CIVU	*Picea abies*	PIAB		
Coronilla varia	COVA	*Picea pungens*	PIPU		
Daucus carota	DACA	*Picea* sp.	PIxx		
Dactylis glomerata	DAGL	*Pinus resinosa*	PIRE		
Dirca palustris	DIPA	*Pinus strobus*	PIST		
Elymus virginicus	ELVI	*Pinus sylvestris*	PISY		
Equisetum sp.	EQxx	*Plantago lanceolata*	PLLA		
Erigeron annuus	ERAN	*Poa alsodes*	POAL		
Fagus grandiflora	FAGR	*Potentilla argentea*	POAR		
Fraxinus Americana	FRAM	*Polygonatum biflorum*	POBI		
Fragaria virginiana	FRVI	*Populus grandidentata*	POGR		
Geranium pusillum	GEPU	*Populus nigra*	PONI		
Glecoma hederacea	GLHE	*Poa pratensis*	POPR		
Gleditsia triacanthos	GLTR	*Potentilla recta*	PORE		
Hamamelis virginiana	HAVI	*Populus tremuloides*	POTR		
Hieracium aurantiacum	HIAU	*Prunus serotina*	PRSE		
Hieracium piloselloides	HIPI	*Pteridium aqlinum*	PTAQ		
Hypericum perforatum	HYPE	*Quercus rubra*	QURU		
Juniperus communis	JUCO	*Ribes cynosbati*	RICY		
Laportea canadensis	LACA	*Robinia pseudoacacia*	ROPS		
Rumex acetosella	RUAC	*Trillium grandiflorum*	TRGR		
Rubus sp.	RUxx	*Trifolium pretense*	TRPR		
Salix sp.	SAxx	*Trifolium repens*	TRRE		
Sambucus pubens	SAPU	*Trifolium* sp.	TRxx		

Appendix C. Survey-wide and sub-regional (sub-Upper Midwest) population trends for 83 species of birds encountered within historic openland portions of Sleeping Bear Dunes National Lakeshore.

Population trends shown are from the U.S. Breeding Bird Survey for 1966 to 2000 (Sauer et al. 2001). Physiographic Stratum 28 = Northern Spruce / Hardwoods; Physiographic Stratum 20 = Great Lakes Transition; Physiographic Stratum 16/17 = Driftless Area and Great Lakes Plain combined. * = Non-significant population trends (P >0.10).

Species	Population Trend (%) (Number of Routes)			
	Survey-wide	Physio. 28	Physio. 20	Physio. 16/17
American crow	1.05	1.65	0.85	1.53
	(3,229)	(288)	(64)	(147)
American goldfinch	-0.39	-0.62*	1.33	1.31
	(2,581)	(283)	(64)	(147)
American kestrel	0.03*	0.38*	-0.86*	1.22
	(2,369)	(174)	(54)	(130)
American robin	0.77	0.16*	-0.06*	1.40
	(3,369)	(294)	(64)	(146)
Baltimore oriole	-0.55	-2.22	-0.54*	-0.37*
	(1,743)	(159)	(64)	(144)
Barn swallow	-0.61	-3.92	-0.24*	0.64
	(3,370)	(266)	(63)	(147)
Black-billed cuckoo	-1.86	-1.24	-0.81*	-2.35
	(1,177)	(175)	(57)	(104)
Black-capped chickadee	1.33	2.47	1.60	3.59
	(1,699)	(290)	(64)	(132)
Brown-headed cowbird	-1.04	-5.64	-2.38	-1.30
	(3,524)	(251)	(64)	(146)
Blue jay	-1.14	0.38*	-0.11*	0.35*
	(2,484)	(293)	(64)	(145)
Brown thrasher	-1.18	-3.14	-1.38	-3.59
	(2,235)	(150)	(60)	(138)
Black-throated blue warbler	0.92*	1.67*	2.33*	No Data
	(436)	(191)	(7)	
Black-throated green warbler	0.06*	-0.04*	9.34	-9.35
	(693)	(274)	(5)	(5)
Blue-winged teal	-0.36*	-2.72*	-2.66	-4.46
	(611)	(29)	(30)	(44)
Bobolink	-1.61	-2.33	-0.23*	-3.92
	(1,212)	(219)	(63)	(140)
Canada goose	10.00	48.40*	16.00	14.07
	(1,289)	(68)	(42)	(98)
Carolina wren	0.89	No Data	No Data	11.93
	(1,387)			(17)
Clay-colored sparrow	-1.10	-1.60*	-0.66*	-4.33*
	(472)	(69)	(40)	(13)
Cedar waxwing	1.36	0.99	0.07*	1.71
	(1,913)	(291)	(63)	(140)

41

Appendix C. Survey-wide and sub-regional (sub-Upper Midwest) population trends for 83 species of birds encountered within historic openland portions of Sleeping Bear Dunes National Lakeshore (continued).

Species	Population Trend (%) (Number of Routes)			
	Survey-wide	Physio. 28	Physio. 20	Physio. 16/17
Chipping sparrow	-0.09*	-0.54*	0.79*	1.94
	(2,864)	(284)	(64)	(1.46)
Common grackle	-1.45	-0.74	-2.18	-3.10
	(2,716)	(281)	(62)	(146)
Connecticut warbler	-1.94	-1.04*	-11.14*	No Data
	(88)	(44)	(5)	
Common raven	2.86	2.64	10.27	No Data
	(1,614)	(282)	(33)	
Common snipe	0.01*	-2.24	0.48*	-2.79*
	(1,118)	(237)	(43)	(25)
Common yellowthroat	-0.30	-0.46*	0.76	0.53*
	(2,897)	(295)	(64)	(144)
Chestnut-sided warbler	-0.69	-0.39*	1.80	5.24*
	(878)	(288)	(58)	(43)
Double-crested cormorant	9.94	15.07	1.51*	15.37
	(420)	(52)	(10)	(13)
Eastern bluebird	2.65	1.00*	3.17	7.48
	(1,919)	(113)	(62)	(131)
Eastern kingbird	-0.95	-1.45	-1.89	-1.96
	(2,643)	(237)	(62)	(145)
Eastern meadowlark	-2.88	-2.66	-2.12	-4.29
	(2,069)	(123)	(59)	(142)
Eastern phoebe	1.16	2.69	2.25	3.11
	(1,909)	(211)	(64)	(132)
Eastern towhee	-1.90	-3.53	-2.07*	-0.24*
	(1,695)	(70)	(49)	(119)
European starling	-0.92	-1.74	-0.62*	-1.41
	(3,394)	(261)	(63)	(146)
Field sparrow	-3.12	-4.05	-2.58	-3.10
	(1,736)	(68)	(53)	(141)
Grasshopper sparrow	-3.71	5.06*	-9.49	-9.44
	(1,513)	(27)	(46)	(107)
Great blue heron	2.36	1.34*	-0.49*	4.80
	(2,255)	(196)	(58)	(135)
Great crested flycatcher	-0.02*	-1.27	-0.24*	0.19*
	(2,186)	(195)	(64)	(144)
Gray catbird	-0.24*	-2.45	-0.07*	0.94
	(2,171)	(238)	(64)	(144)
Green heron	-0.81	-0.45*	-0.67*	-1.24*
	(1,614)	(31)	(47)	(115)
Hairy woodpecker	1.52	3.10	0.12*	-0.67*
	(2,115)	(255)	(58)	(88)
Henslow's sparrow	-7.44	12.48*	-6.09*	-10.06
	(155)	(4)	(14)	(42)
House finch	1.51*	25.60	24.65	23.72
	(2,043)	(44)	(46)	(131)

42

Appendix C. Survey-wide and sub-regional (sub-Upper Midwest) population trends for 83 species of birds encountered within historic openland portions of Sleeping Bear Dunes National Lakeshore (continued).

Species	Population Trend (%) (Number of Routes)			
	Survey-wide	Physio. 28	Physio. 20	Physio. 16/17
House wren	1.08	-0.11*	0.59*	1.28
	(2,253)	(124)	(63)	(144)
Indigo bunting	-0.69	0.18*	-0.29*	0.00*
	(2,026)	(152)	(64)	(144)
Killdeer	-0.33	-3.31	-0.48*	0.56
	(3,298)	(226)	(63)	(146)
Le Conte's sparrow	1.42*	7.66*	-0.15*	No Data
	(182)	(23)	(9)	
Mallard	1.82	1.39*	2.04*	2.17
	(2,135)	(128)	(58)	(136)
Magnolia warbler	1.51	1.46	2.59*	No Data
	(545)	(272)	(8)	
Mourning dove	-0.25	8.27	0.91*	0.42*
	(3,638)	(235)	(64)	(147)
Northern cardinal	0.01*	28.67	5.96	2.17
	(2,027)	(24)	(52)	(146)
Northern flicker	-2.73	-1.03	-4.15	-3.61
	(2,405)	(295)	(61)	(143)
Northern harrier	-0.67*	1.98*	0.68*	2.96*
	(985)	(107)	(38)	(40)
Ovenbird	0.55	-0.03*	1.72	2.87
	(1,456)	(292)	(64)	(81)
Pileated woodpecker	1.45	2.83	6.87	5.31
	(1,776)	(201)	(48)	(40)
Rose-breasted grosbeak	-0.80	-2.07	0.00*	0.72*
	(1,260)	(270)	(63)	(133)
Red-eyed vireo	1.27	1.68	2.63	1.98
	(2,415)	(294)	(64)	(140)
Red-headed woodpecker	-2.47	-6.34	-2.45	-6.31
	(1,236)	(21)	(49)	(114)
Red-tailed hawk	2.92	4.30	4.19	1.77
	(2,859)	(75)	(49)	(132)
Ruby-throated hummingbird	2.49	2.44	4.77	6.84
	(1,465)	(204)	(46)	(76)
Ruffed grouse	-1.90*	0.38*	-1.75*	5.27*
	(531)	(162)	(36)	(12)
Red-winged blackbird	-0.97	-2.10	-0.50*	-1.60
	(3,526)	(283)	(64)	(146)
Savannah sparrow	-0.53	-1.13	-1.95	-2.14
	(1,629)	(234)	(60)	(140)
Scarlet tanager	-0.18*	-0.83*	1.93	2.10
	(1,340)	(195)	(59)	(109)
Sedge wren	3.01	2.02	3.01	-0.63*
	(361)	(63)	(46)	(66)
Sora	1.29	0.09*	-3.10	-1.08*
	(465)	(36)	(28)	(16)

Appendix C. Survey-wide and sub-regional (sub-Upper Midwest) population trends for 83 species of birds encountered within historic openland portions of Sleeping Bear Dunes National Lakeshore (continued).

Species	Population Trend (%) (Number of Routes)			
	Survey-wide	Physio. 28	Physio. 20	Physio. 16/17
Song sparrow	-0.50 (2,567)	-1.26 (294)	0.56* (64)	0.30* (146)
Swamp sparrow	1.42 (787)	0.85* (249)	5.87 (52)	-0.43* (77)
Tree swallow	0.47* (1,992)	-1.47 (283)	2.78 (64)	3.11 (139)
Turkey vulture	1.49 (2,017)	15.54 (32)	5.35* (20)	7.46 (87)
Upland sandpiper	0.99 (609)	2.75 (41)	-2.97 (33)	-3.87 (47)
Vesper sparrow	-0.89 (1,612)	-3.09 (125)	-3.33 (57)	-4.01 (132)
Western meadowlark	-0.62 (1606)	-3.50 (37)	-8.65 (36)	-9.38 (77)
White-breasted nuthatch	2.19 (1,831)	0.51* (142)	2.43 (61)	0.52* (135)
White-crowned sparrow	-1.59 (318)	No Data	No Data	No Data
Whip-poor-will	-1.81 (491)	0.25* (39)	-2.78* (20)	2.33* (14)
Wild turkey	12.29 (774)	20.33 (7)	10.42* (31)	40.23 (50)
Wood duck	5.19 (1,144)	9.80 (74)	5.91 (43)	2.86 (102)
Wood thrush	-1.86 (1,776)	-4.89 (181)	-1.13* (55)	0.95 (133)
White-throated sparrow	-0.80 (702)	-1.14 (295)	-0.56* (38)	3.50* (8)
Yellow-bellied sapsucker	-0.19* (645)	-1.09 (260)	7.87 (46)	6.77* (15)
Yellow palm warbler	4.40 (58)	4.01 (54)	No Data	No Data
Yellow warbler	0.52 (2,480)	0.22* (265)	1.75 (63)	2.00 (142)

NPS D-128, January 2009

National Park Service
U.S. Department of the Interior

Natural Resource Program Center
1201 Oakridge Drive, Suite 150
Fort Collins, CO 80525

www.nature.nps.gov

EXPERIENCE YOUR AMERICA ™